PRAY LIKE A GIRL

# Pray Like A Girl

CAROLINE S VAIGAFA-GALLULO

# Contents

| | | |
|---|---|---|
| *Dedication* | | ix |
| 1 | Why this Book | 2 |
| 2 | The Myth of Pretty Prayers | 6 |
| 3 | How Women in the Bible Model Prayer | 13 |
| 4 | Personal Note My Own Awkward Prayers | 22 |
| | **HANNAH** | 30 |
| 5 | The Story of Hannah | 32 |
| 6 | Hannah's Ugly Prayer | 41 |
| 7 | Lessons from Hannah's Prayer | 49 |
| | **MARY MOTHER OF JESUS** | 57 |
| 8 | The Story of Mary | 59 |
| 9 | Mary's Magnificat | 66 |
| 10 | Lessons from Mary's Prayer | 73 |
| | **DEBORAH** | 78 |
| 11 | The Story of Deborah | 80 |
| 12 | Deborah's Song of Victory | 89 |
| 13 | Lessons from Deborah's Prayer | 95 |
| | **ESTHER** | 101 |
| 14 | The Story of Esther | 103 |
| 15 | Esther's Fasting and Prayer | 114 |

| 16 | Lessons from Esther's Prayer | 127 |
|---|---|---|
| | HAGAR | 134 |
| 17 | The Story of Hagar | 136 |
| 18 | Hagar's Wilderness Whispers | 150 |
| 19 | Lesson's from Hagar's Prayer | 160 |
| | ANNA THE PROPHETESS | 173 |
| 20 | The Story of Anna | 175 |
| 21 | Anna's Temple Prayer Life | 183 |
| 22 | Lessons from Anna's Prayer | 191 |
| | SYROPHOENICIAN WOMAN | 196 |
| 23 | The Story of the Syrophoenician Woman | 198 |
| 24 | Her Bold Plea for Her Daughter | 206 |
| 25 | Lessons from Syrophoenician Woman's Prayer | 216 |
| | THE BLEEDING WOMAN | 225 |
| 26 | The Story of the Bleeding Woman | 227 |
| 27 | The Bleeding Woman's Silent Prayer of Touch | 234 |
| 28 | Lessons from the Bleeding Woman's Prayer | 245 |
| | LEAH | 250 |
| 29 | The Story of Leah | 252 |
| 30 | Leah's Heart in the Names of Her Children | 262 |
| 31 | Lessons from Leah's Prayer | 270 |
| | MARY MAGDALENE | 276 |
| 32 | The Story of Mary Magdalene | 278 |
| 33 | Mary Magdalene's Brokenhearted Prayer | 290 |
| 34 | Lessons from Mary Magdalene's Prayer | 298 |
| | CONCLUSION | 304 |

## ~ *VII*

| | | |
|---|---|---|
| 35 | Why Praying Like a Girl Matters | 306 |
| 36 | Your Prayers Count Even the Messy Ones | 315 |

Copyright © 2025 by Caroline S Vaigafa-Gallulo
All rights reserved. No part of this book may be reproduced in any manner whatsoever without written permission except in the case of brief quotations embodied in critical articles and reviews.
First Printing, 2025

I dedicate this book to my daughters and their sons and daughters, and to my sons and their daughters and sons. My prayer for you is that you will discover the true power of a relationship with God through prayer—that you will learn you can lean on Him in every season, with every joy and every ache.

My prayer for you, dear reader, is that somewhere in these pages you will find yourself having a moment with God—a moment that may come with deep sobs and snot-filled tissues. Because those are the moments that change everything. They reset me when I've lost my way. They reconnect me to Jesus.

God's peace is not only the quiet, restful kind. It is also a fire-building, heart-inferno kind of peace that ignites new things inside you. I pray you find that. And don't worry—everyone may think you're crazy, your family may suggest new hobbies (haha), but you will know in your spirit that God has set something special aside for you. It's up to you whether you take it up.

# Thank you

A special thank you goes to Pastor Luke Merriman, his wife Lauren, and their amazing kids. Pastor Luke was the first person to put me on a platform to share a message—and fittingly, it was a Mother's Day message on Hannah. To be honest, I can hardly remember what I said, but I will always remember the patience and care Pastor showed in helping me prepare. At the time, I wanted to impress people and preach like him, or like one of the great evangelists.

In reality, I think I may have bored everyone to death. It took me eight years to realize that God wasn't asking me to be anyone else—He called me to teach as I am: a storyteller, a joker, but always dedicated to His truth.

How incredibly thankful I am to him and his family, for his attention and leadership. Up until then, I never thought I could ever share anything noteworthy—anything worth listening too. It might as well have been a dream. But the moment I was presented the opportunity, it lit a new fire in my heart: *I want to do this, and I want to give it my all.* I can never thank you all enough. This book may never have come about without your guidance, inspiration as an amazing pastor and family, impressionable teacher, and for being wonderful, Jesus-loving human beings.

May God Bless you all

# Chapter 1

# Why this Book

**The Day I Realized My Prayers Were Terrible (And Why That's Okay)**

*OR: HOW SHOWER CRIES & UGLY PRAYERS CHANGED EVERYTHING*

I used to think prayer was a spiritual talent show. Some people just had the gift—the soaring, poetic words, the flawless Scripture recall, the ability to pray for twenty minutes without once saying "um" or trailing off into existential panic. Then there was me. My prayers sounded like a text message to a friend who might be ignoring me:

*"Hey, God. It's me again. So, uh, today was... a lot. I have no idea what I'm doing. Help?"*

I spent years convinced I was doing it wrong. I'd hear those stunning prayers in church or on Christian podcasts—the ones that sounded like they were transcribed straight from heaven—and I'd shrink a little. My inner critic would whisper: *Why can't you pray like that?*

But here's the funny thing: The more I tried to *perform* my prayers, the less I actually prayed.

## "Prayer Room" Confessions

Let me set the scene: I'm in the shower. (Yes, my *prayer closet* is a shower stall, and no, you don't get to judge me. Elijah had his cave, David had his fields, and I? I have hot water, steam, and the occasional shampoo bottle falling on my head like a divine wake-up call.)

So there I am—standing under scalding water (because apparently suffering equals holiness and my inner soul loves the hot water even if my epidermis resents it), and I'm trying to pray. Not just *any* prayer, mind you, but one of those *beautiful* prayers. The kind you hear from—

The prayer team warrior at church (who somehow always knows Psalm 91 and Isaiah 40 *by memory* while I'm Googling "short prayers for desperate people").

The perfectly poised YouTuber who prays like she's narrating a Bible audiobook (*"Father God, we just come before You today in humble adoration—"*). Me? *"Hi, God... it's me. Uhh... you know. Help?"*

That one lady at Bible study who drops a tear at just the right moment in her prayer, while I'm over here choking up because my coffee was too hot.

And let me tell you, the harder I tried to *sound* spiritual, the more my brain short-circuited. I'd start planning my prayers mid-prayer—*Wait, what's a better word for 'desperate'? Should I throw in a 'hallelujah' here? Oh no, I forgot to repent first—* until my "prayer" sounded more like a bad audition for *Sermon Idol*.

## The Birth of an Ugly Prayer Revolution

Then God, in His infinite wisdom (and probably cosmic sense of humor), dragged me down a biblical rabbit hole. One day, I stumbled upon Hagar—abandoned in the desert, sobbing over her dying son. No eloquence, just raw despair: *"Don't let me watch my child die."* (Genesis 21:16)

Then came Hannah, drunk on grief, lips flapping silently in the tabernacle until the priest thought she was wasted (1 Samuel 1:13). Leah, screaming through childbirth, naming her kids after her heartbreak (*"Maybe NOW my husband will love me!"* Genesis 29:32). The bleeding woman, barging through a crowd to *touch Jesus' hem* (Mark 5:28). No polished speeches—just desperation, snot, and unapologetic need.

And that's when it hit me like a falling shampoo bottle:

God doesn't want your performance. He wants your *panic*.
He doesn't need perfect words. He wants your *ugly cry*.
Your prayer doesn't have to sound like a worship leader's. It can sound like a sleep-deprived mom muttering, *"I can't do this—help."*

## The Freedom of Praying Like a Girl

You know what *praying like a girl* really means? It means praying like you've got nothing to prove.

Pray like you're drunk. (Looking at you, Hannah.)

Pray like you're bleeding. (Literally, if necessary.)

Pray like you're naming your kid "God Hears Me Because My Husband Doesn't." (Leah, you dramatic queen.)

Pray like you're in the shower, where no one can hear you but God—and honestly, He's heard worse. Shower is always good for crying prayers, cause who's gonna know? Great for clearing snot from running down your face too.

This book isn't about *pretty prayers*. It's about the messy, gutsy, downright awkward ones that *actually changed history*. Because God doesn't grade on grammar. He leans in for the tears, the laughter, the *"I don't know what to say but here's my chaos."*

So take a deep breath. Stop rehearsing. Toss the prayer-performance anxiety away.

And let's pray like girls.

*(Cue shower steam as holy ambiance.)*

## Questions for You (Because This Isn't a Lecture, It's a Chat):

1. Where's your weirdest/most honest "prayer closet"? (Car? Laundry room? Behind the fridge?)
2. Ever caught yourself *editing* your prayers mid-prayer? Spill the awkward.
3. Which biblical woman's prayer style do you *wish* you could borrow? (I'm voting for Esther—girl fasted for *three days* before even *asking* for help. Legend.)

# Chapter 2

# The Myth of Pretty Prayers

**WHY GOD PREFERS YOUR SNOTTY SOB-FEST OVER POETIC PERFORMANCES**

### The Prayer Olympics (And Why You Don't Need a Gold Medal)

Let's play a game. Name the most *awe-inspiring* prayer you've ever heard.

Was it:

The pastor who prayed for 20 minutes without taking a breath?

The small group leader whose intercession sounded like a Shakespearean soliloquy?

That one auntie who says *"Amen"* like she's signing a legal document?

Now—name the most *honest* prayer you've ever heard.
*(Crickets? Yeah. That's the problem.)*

We've been sold a lie: That prayer is a performance. That God grades on eloquence. That the "best" prayers sound like they belong in a hymnal.

But here's the truth: The prayers that move heaven aren't pretty. They're desperate.

**Case Study: The Two Prayers of Luke 18**

Jesus literally told a parable about this. Meet our contestants:

**Prayer #1: The Pharisee**

- *"God, I thank You that I am not like other people—robbers, evildoers, adulterers—or even like this tax collector."* (Luke 18:11)
- Translation: *"Check out my spiritual résumé!"*
- Delivery**:** Pristine. Poised. Probably smelled like sandalwood incense.

**Prayer #2: The Tax Collector**

- *"God, have mercy on me, a sinner."* (Luke 18:13)
- Translation: *"I'm a wreck. Help."*
- Delivery: Eyes down, chest pounding, possibly hyperventilating.

**And the winner is...** the guy who didn't even finish his sentence.

Jesus' verdict: *"This man went home justified before God."* (Luke 18:14)

Mic drop.

Here's the thing about prayer: pretty prayers are usually about us, and ugly prayers are about God. You know the pretty kind—"Lord, I humbly come before You, acknowledging Your sovereignty..." which is basically church-speak for, *"Everybody please notice how theologically sound I am right now."* Then there's the ugly kind, the one that usually comes out between sobs or through clenched teeth: *"God, I can't do this without You."* One is a performance. The other is pure surrender. And spoiler alert—God's not grading our grammar. He's after the messy, heart-spilling, can't-do-this-alone prayers every single time.

## Pretty Prayers Edit. Ugly Prayers Bleed.

Ever cried so hard your nose ran? Congrats—you've prayed like Hannah. Ever screamed into a pillow? Welcome to David's Psalm Club. Ever whispered *"I don't even know what to say"*? That's the Holy Spirit groaning for you (Romans 8:26).

God doesn't need your words polished. He wants your heart exposed.

Pretty prayers impress people. Ugly prayers move God. Look at Elijah. On Mount Carmel he's basically the prophet version of a rock star—calling down fire from heaven, trash-talking the prophets of Baal, and praying this perfectly scripted "Show them You're God" prayer. It's dramatic, it's cinematic, it's the kind of prayer you'd post on Instagram if you could.

Fast-forward one chapter and the same guy is hiding under a broom tree saying, *"I just want to die."* No theatrics. No fire-calling. Just raw burnout and despair. Guess which prayer got answered with fire from heaven...and which one got answered with

## The Ugly Truth About "Pretty" Prayers

Let me introduce you to the three fatal flaws of performed spirituality:

<u>They Focus on Human Approval</u>
Every time we polish our prayers for public consumption, we've switched audiences. It's no longer about talking to God—it's about impressing the people listening.

<u>They Create Spiritual Imposter Syndrome</u>
When we only hear perfect prayers, we start believing: "If I can't pray like that, I shouldn't pray at all." And suddenly, we stop praying completely.

<u>They Filter Out Real Need</u>
Ever notice how "pretty" prayers often skip over the messy stuff? No one thanks God for their anxiety meds or weeps over their failing marriage in polished King James English.

Just because you didn't ask but here is the The Hall of Fame for Ugly Prayers

1. Moses: The "I Quit" Prayer "If this is how You're going to treat me, just kill me now." (Numbers 11:15) God's response: Sent help (and quail. So much quail).
2. Jonah: The "I'm Pouting in a Fish" Prayer "I'd rather die than see these people saved." (Jonah 4:3) God's response: "You okay, bro?" (Jonah 4:9, paraphrased)

3. Jesus: The "Take This Cup" Prayer "Father, if possible, don't make me do this." (Luke 22:42) God's response: Strengthened Him through an angel (Luke 22:43).

Notice a pattern? The messier the prayer, the bigger the miracle.

## How to Pray Ugly: A Friendly Guide

Alright, let's chat about how to pray without all the fuss, shall we? Here's a simple way to make your prayer life a whole lot messier—and honestly, more real!

Step 1: Ditch the Fancy Words
First off, forget fancy vocabulary! God's not grading your words. Seriously, sometimes a simple *"Help"* is all you need. Keep it real!

Step 2: Let Those Tears Flow
Got tears? Fantastic! And if you've got snot bubbles too? Even better! Remember, the altar isn't a place to look perfect—it's where you can be completely yourself.

Step 3: Pray Like Nobody's Watching (Because Honestly, It's Just You and God)
You know that feeling when you're at church and think everyone's judging your prayers? Forget that! Church isn't a stage show. If you're all worried about what others think, you might just be missing the point. It's all about connecting with God!

Step 4: Borrow a Prayer from the Bible

Feeling a bit off? That's okay! Here are some prayers you can swipe:

- Too angry? Try Psalm 109.
- Feeling scared? Check out Psalm 56:3.
- Feeling numb? Remember this: Mark 9:24 says, *"I believe; help my unbelief!"*

So go ahead—let those prayers be as messy as they need to be!

## Your Turn: The Ugly Prayer Challenge

This week, try this:

1. Find your "ugly prayer" place (closet, car, shower, wherever).
2. Set a timer for 60 seconds.
3. Pray *one* raw, unfiltered sentence. No edits. No fancy words.

Example:

*"God, I'm so mad at You right now."*
*"I don't know if You're even listening."*
*"I'm scared."*
*"I Truly don't even know what to say right now, can you help?"*

Then... wait. See what happens when you stop performing and start *being*.

## Discussion Questions (Because We're Still Chatting, Not Preaching):

1. **What's the "prettiest" prayer you've ever heard?** Did it inspire you... or intimidate you?
2. **Share an "ugly prayer" you've prayed.** (No judgment—we've all been there.) Besides this is a book and I can't actually hear what you say, so it's all good in the sister - hood.
3. **Which biblical "ugly prayer" do you wish you could pray more boldly?** (I'm partial to Elijah's *"Kill me now"* vibe but I won't lie, so many times i wanna wrestle like Jacob, although the whole Hip thing has me having second thoughts.)

God doesn't want your eloquence. He wants your *everything.* So go ahead—pray ugly. Heaven's listening.
*(And if you cry... well, that's just holy water.)*

# Chapter 3

# How Women in the Bible Model Prayer

***O****R: WHY GOD KEEPS PICKING THE "UNQUALIFIED" TO SHAKE HISTORY*

Okay, let's be real for a second. If we were casting a biblical prayer dream team, most of us wouldn't pick the women God actually used. I mean, let's look at the resumes:

There's Hannah - the tipsy-looking temple crier who got mistaken for the town drunk. Mary - the pregnant teenager with an impossible story not even her fiancé believed at first. The Bleeding Woman - ceremonially unclean just for existing in her own body. And my personal favorite, the Syrophoenician woman who basically told Jesus, "Excuse me sir, but you're being racist right now" (Matt 15:27, Sunday School teacher-approved version).

Not exactly who you'd invite to lead your women's prayer brunch, am I right? And yet—here's the kicker—these are the exact women whose prayers literally changed the trajectory of salvation history. Let that sink in while I refill my coffee.

## The Unexpected Avengers of Prayer

Let me paint you a picture: Heaven's "War Room"—where world-changing prayers get strategized. You'd expect to see all the spiritual giants in there, right? Moses with his staff. Elijah with his dramatic showdowns. Paul with his 10-page theological prayers.

But when the angelic intern pulls back the curtain, who's actually sitting at the table?

- A barren woman drunk-crying in the temple
- A teenage girl saying yes to societal ruin
- A desert runaway sobbing over her dying son
- A menstruating outcast touching a rabbi's robe
- An 80-something widow who won't shut up in the temple

The mightiest prayers in Scripture didn't come from professionals. They came from women society ignored, dismissed, or straight-up pitied.

And friend? That means *your* messy prayers might be next in line to move mountains.

## The All-Star Roster of Prayer Warriors (Who Didn't Know They Were Warriors)

Hannah: The "They Thought I Was Wasted Sober" Prayer (1 Samuel 1)

Hannah's story is legendary, and not because everything looked put together. She was barren in a culture where motherhood basically equaled your worth. To make things worse, her husband's other wife, Peninnah—whose name, I swear, must translate to "worst roommate ever"—never let her forget it. And when Hannah finally broke down in the temple, even the priest assumed she was drunk. That's right: stone-cold sober, just ugly-crying so hard that Eli mistook her for tipsy.

Her prayer wasn't polished. It was tears more than words. It was vows made in emotional desperation—"Take my kid, just help me!"—the kind of thing that sounds like the sleep-deprived bargaining every mom has whispered at 3 a.m. She didn't even finish with a tidy "Amen." But somehow, that raw outpouring of anguish was exactly what heaven was waiting for. God answered with Samuel, the prophet who would grow up to anoint kings and change Israel's story forever. Hannah's messy, misunderstood prayer literally altered the course of history.

She prayed "out of her great anguish"_ (v. 16) — and heaven ANSWERED with Samuel, the prophet who'd anoint kings.

Mary: The "Hold My Wine, I'm Changing History" Prayer (Luke 1)

Mary was probably about fourteen, just engaged, and dreaming of a quiet little life with Joseph—maybe baking bread, maybe raising kids, definitely not planning on becoming the mother of the Messiah. Then boom: she's suddenly pregnant, in a culture where "suddenly pregnant" could get you stoned (and not the fun kind). Everything about her situation screamed disaster, yet somehow she didn't fall apart.

Instead, her prayer was shockingly simple: "Let it be as You've said." No bargaining. No "But what if people talk?" Just instant surrender. And then she launches into the Magnificat—a prophetic rap so fierce it still gives goosebumps two thousand years later. That was Mary's secret: she wasn't worried about her reputation, she was focused on God's plan. Her indifference to human approval made her the perfect vessel to carry the Savior who would rewrite history.

Her *indifference to human approval* made her the perfect vessel for Messiah.

The Bleeding Woman: The "No Words, Just Reckless Faith" Prayer (Mark 5)

The bleeding woman had been suffering for twelve years—twelve years of being labeled "unclean," which meant religious exile on top of the medical nightmare. She was broke from paying doctors who couldn't help and had basically been pushed to live in the shadows. Everyone expected her to keep quiet and stay hidden.

But her prayer wasn't words—it was action. She didn't schedule an appointment or craft a speech; she just pushed through the crowd and grabbed the hem of Jesus' robe. In that moment, she technically broke about fifteen religious laws, but desperation doesn't check rulebooks. And instead of scolding her, Jesus stopped, turned, and called her "Daughter." After more than a decade of being ignored, nameless, and excluded, God Himself gave her a name and a place in His family. Desperate faith wins over polished words every single time.

Desperate faith defeats polished words EVERY TIME

## When God Uses the Least Instagram-Worthy Prayers

I'll never forget the first time I truly *got* Hannah's story. There I was, ugly crying in the shower again (my personal prayer closet) after a particularly brutal week, i just felt like my life was falling apart, my marriage, everything i work hard for just seemed to dwindle, then id catch up with friends and family, who had asked me to pray for them and they are seeing God work in their life, living Pinterest-perfect lives, sharing their beautifully crafted prayer journals, Homes and dressed up even though they have toddlers etc. Meanwhile, my life was sweat pants and my husbands shirts, hair in a bun, depressed and oh my prayer life consisted of hastily scribbled sticky notes that usually said things like:

"God - WHY ?? As I chuck a toddler tantrum and oh Also plz let me find matching socks."

Then I re-read Hannah's story and nearly spit out my lukewarm coffee. This woman shows up at church looking like she'd been day drinking (1 Sam 1:13), gets scolded by the priest, and instead of making excuses, basically says:

"Oh honey, I'm not drunk—I'm just pouring out my messy, desperate heart to God. Maybe you should try it sometime." (1 Sam 1:15, Taylor paraphrase)

And guess what? God heard *that* prayer over every polished religious performance happening in the temple that day.

This all became hilariously real when my friend texted me last month she was having a Hannah meltdown moment

Some of the most powerful prayers happen:

- While scrubbing vomit out of car seats
- In the store parking lot after losing it with your kids
- During another sleepless night with a newborn when all you can whisper is "Jesus, take the wheel...and the baby" I just need five minutes.
- Trying hard to turn the other cheek at work.
- Getting mad cause you thought God would click his magic fingers and fix everything ....and he didn't.

These aren't less holy than the Instagrammable morning devotionals—they might actually be more holy because they're 100% real.

## The Bleeding Woman Who Said 'Screw the Rules'

Can we talk about my girl in Mark 5? Twelve YEARS of bleeding made her untouchable in Jewish culture. She wasn't supposed to be in crowds. Definitely wasn't supposed to touch a rabbi.

But desperation breeds holy audacity. She thinks: *"If I can just touch His laundry, maybe I'll stop bleeding through all my pants."* (Mark 5:28, Modern Woman Translation)

What kills me is how Jesus responds. Instead of scolding her for breaking purity laws, He turns it into a teachable moment for the disciples:

*"Hold up! Someone just drew supernatural power from me. Watch and learn, boys."* (v. 30, Casual Bible Translation)

Then—get this—He calls her **"Daughter."** After twelve years of being called "Unclean," the God of the universe gives her a new name over breakfast.

## Your Turn: Finding Your Unorthodox Prayer Style

Maybe you're not a Hannah-style ugly crier. That's cool! That's me too. I'll cry with you most of the time too or if i see a really cute dog or a llama apparently. The biblical women show us multiple ways to bring raw faith:

The Mary Method: When life gives you a crisis pregnancy (metaphorical or literal), break into spontaneous worship rap (Luke 1:46-55). Extra points if you do it while folding laundry.

The Deborah Approach: Lead worship *and* warfare (Judges 4-5). Warning: May require telling reluctant men where to go (Judges 4:6).

The Rachel Move: When you're jealous of your sister's blessings, just yell at God about it (Gen 30:1). He can handle your honesty.

## Why This Should Make You Giddy

Here's the scandalous truth: God seems to prefer prayers from women society considers too much. Too emotional. Too bold. Too unstable. Too loud.

While the religious gatekeepers were polishing their public prayers, these women were:

[ ] Following the rules
[ ✓ ] Following Jesus

Your messy, desperate, unorthodox prayers don't disqualify you—they might actually be your superpower.

*** 

## Let's Get Practical

- Pray where you *actually* are (mentally/spiritually/physically) not where you "should" be
- Ask God what your strength is in prayer. Keep it real and honest.

So go ahead—touch the hem of His garment today. He's not grossed out by your mess. He's leaning in closer to hear you.

Even if (especially if) you're currently:

- Covered in baby spit up
- Late for work
- Wearing yesterday's yoga pants
- Emotionally a train wreck
- Just don't know what is wrong with you today, this week, this month, this year

He's in the chaos with you. Now *that's* Good News.

P.S. Next time someone side-eyes your unconventional prayers, just hit them with this truth bomb: "The women who changed history didn't wait for permission to approach God—they crashed the party." Drop mic. Walk away. or maybe better advice would be to just pray about them and let God do God?

# Chapter 4

# Personal Note My Own Awkward Prayers

**OR: HOW GOD USED BATHROOM FLOORS, SNOTTY TEARS, & DESPERATE GROANS**

### Confessions of a Hot Mess Prayer Warrior

If prayer were an Olympic sport, I wouldn't be the gymnast scoring perfect 10s. I'd be the girl who trips over her own feet, faceplants on the mat, and somehow *still* gets the gold medal because—plot twist—God apparently loves chaos prayers best.

Let me take you on a tour of my *greatest prayer fails* (that somehow ended up being my greatest faith wins).

### Single Mom Rage-Prayers & Divine Detox

Me. Early 20s. Two babies barely over a year apart. Working two jobs. Sleeping approximately 17 minutes per night. And carrying enough anger to power a small city. My prayer life sounded something like:

*"God, if You're up there, You see this nonsense, right? Either help me or get out of the way, because I WILL fight everyone You created today."*

I had perfected the art of *spiritual deforestation*—if you weren't actively helping me survive, I was cutting you out of my life like overgrown jungle vines. Family? Gone.
 Friends? Bye. Cashier who gave me side-eye when my toddler had a meltdown? Believe me, she felt my wrath through telepathy.

Then one day—probably while hiding in a bathroom stall crying—I prayed the dumbest prayer of my life:

*"Fine. If You won't smite my enemies, at least stop letting me be my own worst enemy."*

And slowly (SO SLOWLY, like divine-molasses slow), God started weeding *me* out of *my* life. Not the people I'd cut off—the bitterness *in me* that made me think I had to be both sword and shield all the time, he taught me he was both and I still had to fight, but i had to fight face down.. in prayer.

Now, decades later? I reunited with family I'd sworn off. Apologized to friends I'd ghosted. And—miracle of miracles—actually let people help me without assuming they were judging my failed-mom moments.

Sometimes the prayer God answers isn't *"Fix them!"* but *"Okay fine... fix me."*

## Divine Sleepovers on the Bathroom Floor

Here's a fun childhood memory: Me at 12 years old, sitting on the bathroom floor at midnight, shower running (not because I was bathing, but because running water was the only sound loud enough to mask my panic attacks).

Backstory: Survival mode was my default setting growing up. So when nighttime terrors hit, or the abuse was particularly bad that day, the bathroom became my safe space. I'd curl up against the tub, shaking, crying, praying nonsense like:

*"I don't wanna die tonight. Please don't let me die tonight. Why won't anyone help me? Get me out of here. I can't do this anymore"*

And here's the weirdest part—every. single. time., I'd wake up hours later, stiff-necked but *peaceful*, slumped against the toilet like some sort of traumatized Cinderella.

Always around 2 or 3 AM. Always right when the house was finally silent.

It took me thirty years to realize:

*"Oh. That wasn't just exhaustion knocking me out. That was God putting me back together enough to survive another day."*

Like supernatural chloroform for my PTSD. Who knew? Sometime, God doesn't get you out of the mess, but he is certainly right there in the middle of it with you.

## The 'Everything Is On Fire' Miracle Week

Fast-forward to adulthood. Few years ago, my life decided to imitate a Netflix disaster movie:

- **House?** Gone.
- **Car?** Deceased.
- **Bank account?** A haunting void.
- **Mental stability?** Laughable concept.
- **Phone?** Bahbumm Adios

One particularly glamorous shower cry session went like this:

*[Sobbing violently]* "God, WHAT IS THE POINT OF ANY OF THIS?? I CAN'T EVEN—" [Sniffle] "—afford Tissues now, apparently!"

I ended up finding myself sobbing and singing praise songs in my now , non working vehicles, just over and over and over again like a made woman.

Then—like God handed the universe a *"Fix Her Life"* checklist—the miracles started rolling in:

Monday: Found a rental house approved *same day* (Landlords: "We never do this but...")
Tuesday: Random friend texts *"Hey, Found a car on Facebook ?"*
Wednesday: Phone company approves me for a plan despite trash credit ("How??")
Thursday: Mysterious superannuation letter falls out of my glovebox—exact amount needed
Friday: Friends of Friends shows up unannounced with moving boxes *and tissues* ("I just felt led")

By Sunday? I was sitting in my new living room 8 hours away, surrounded by half-unpacked chaos, eating takeout off paper plates, my 2 traumatized kids and crazy 16 dogs, whispering:

*"So... You do like me."*

## Why My Ugly Prayers Worked Better Than My Pretty Ones

Let me clarify something here, i am in no way saying your Ugly prayers or Pretty prayers for that matter are going to work and you are going to get the answer to every problem you face. If that is what Prayer is like for you, You may need to rethink the purpose of prayer. Prayer is about getting close to God and yes sharing our problems, dreams and aspirations is a part of that friendship. God openly welcomes you to share everything with him Remember the "But in everything pray." (Abbreviated Philippians 4:6) But he didn't say, the good things or the bad things or when you want to. but in every Situation, Good, Bad, the ugly.

Looking back, here's what I've learned:

### 1. God Specializes in Bathroom Floor Theology

Your most *undignified* prayers? His favorite. Bonus points if you're:

- Sitting on linoleum or hard tiles
- Covered in questionable fluids
- Not even using full sentences
- Loves groans and nonverbal conjunction

2. **Miracles Love Company**

My biggest breakthroughs *always* came when:

- I was too tired to pretend
- I was too honest and too much of a problem to care how I looked or what anyone thought at that moment
- Too broke to "help God out" and be the answer or come up with a redemption plan myself
- Too humiliated to care who knew

3. **Healing Comes in Weird Packaging**

That kid crying herself to sleep hugging a toilet? She's now:

- Healing relationships she once burned - Married, altogether we have 9 kids (2 in heaven) and at this point 5 grandchildren.. never thought that would happen
- Writing books about prayer (LOL the irony)
- Still praying weird shower prayers with snot


Let's get practical:

1. **Find Your Battle Station**

Mine's the shower. Maybe yours is:

- The driver's seat of your parked car
- Behind the locked laundry room door
- That one Starbucks bathroom stall noone uses

It doesn't matter where it is, just make it your own and make it about you and God. That's it. No audience, no filters, just raw time with the ultimate friend.

## 2. **Practice Ugly Honesty**

Try praying:

- Angry: *"I'm furious at You about..."*
- Skeptical: *"I don't believe You'll help but here's my list..."*
- Exhausted: *[Wordless groaning accepted and encouraged]*

God doesn't want our filtered emotions, he wants us honest even when that means we just don't see it or agree. It's hard trusting God's plan if you can not be first, be honest about how uncomfortable it is, especially when you see it going towards some scary cliffhanger. And yes, its easy to remind ourselves, God's got a plan, but sometimes we also need to be honest and say hey i hate this right now. See when we keep this in, we allow footholds to be placed on our lives, we allow thoughts to creep in. But disclosing and surrendering it all to God, allows him to work through it with you. It may not always look like the way you want it too, but my greatest lessons and breakthroughs have always been when I've been down and honest with God.

## 3. **Look Back & Connect Dots**

Where did "coincidences" line up after desperate prayers?

I feel one of the things we always forget in our prayer life is to think back. Think back to that prayer you cried out when you prayed and hoped you had enough for shopping and somehow you just had enough. Then life goes on and we forget.

But sitting back and seeing how God has moved in your life and answered prayers that you are now currently living in, is the ultimate moment of growth and trust.

I feel like there is a reason why God told the Israelite, remember this. (see Joshua 4:6-7, Exodus 12:14)

We grow in our relationship with God when we remember all these amazing things he has done, whether big or small, they all mean something, and they all connect the dots to where you are now.

If my prayer journey teaches anything, it's this:

**God isn't waiting for you to "get good" at prayer—He's waiting for you to get *real*.**

So go ahead.

Cry on your bathroom floor. Yell in your shower. Send Him that rage-text prayer. Praise even when its crazy. Ask for a Hug. And Thank him for all the times he showed up.

He can handle it.

Actually—He *prefers* it.

*(You will see me say that a lot. It's just a reminder. Now pass the tissues.)*

# HANNAH

*"In her deep anguish Hannah prayed to the Lord, weeping bitterly."*
— 1 Samuel 1:10

# Chapter 5

# The Story of Hannah

***O**R: HOW BEING MISTAKEN FOR THE VILLAGE DRUNK CHANGED HISTORY*

*"In her deep anguish Hannah prayed to the Lord, weeping bitterly."* — 1 Samuel 1:10

### Welcome to Hannah's World (AKA Ancient Israel's Messiest Drama)

Before we dive in, let's set the stage properly. Imagine you're living in 1100 BC Israel - no electricity, no DoorDash, and absolutely no therapy for your emotional trauma. This was Hannah's reality.

The hills of Ephraim were alive that year with the sounds of pilgrims climbing the road to Shiloh. Families pressed together, their voices rising in psalms as they carried lambs for sacrifice, oil and grain offerings, baskets of figs. At the heart of this yearly rhythm stood the tabernacle, its curtains weathered but sacred, a meeting place between heaven and earth.

Among the travelers was Elkanah with his two wives, Peninnah and Hannah. Having two wives, should already tell you that probably won't be as symbiotic as you would think. At first glance, their household looked blessed. Peninnah bustled about with her children clinging to her skirts, their laughter carrying across the camp. Hannah, however, walked in quiet dignity, her hands empty. To passersby, the difference was obvious: one woman surrounded by life, the other shadowed by barrenness.

## Three Key Things You Need to Know About Her Culture:

In Hannah's world, baby-making wasn't a side note to life — it was the whole career path. Sons were basically your retirement fund, the ones who would grow up to inherit land and make sure you didn't starve in your old age. Daughters weren't exactly wasted space either; they came with dowry potential, a kind of built-in bank account to bargain with when it came to alliances and family security. But barrenness? That was a financial disaster in slow motion. It wasn't just the ache of an empty cradle — it was the looming fear of being tossed aside, replaced, or left behind. In a culture where legacy lived and died in the womb, Hannah's empty arms made her a public target.

And then came the marriage drama. Polygamy might have been stamped with a big "technically legal" seal, but that didn't make it easy. Think *Sister Wives,* only trade the perfectly staged suburban homes for dusty fields, mismatched tents, and way more goats. Elkanah, her husband, wasn't breaking any divine rules by taking on a second wife, but relationally? Spiritually?

He was failing the vibe check spectacularly. Nothing says "romantic tension" like sharing your home — and your husband — with a woman who just so happens to be a baby-making factory.

Every year, the whole family would pile into Shiloh for the annual feast, and if you've ever sat through an awkward holiday dinner, multiply it by ten. The festival was like Christmas, Thanksgiving, and church camp all rolled into one — joyful songs, bustling crowds, roasted meat on every corner, and the smell of sacrifices drifting through the air. The men portioned out the offerings with pride, families sat in circles eating and laughing, and for most people it was the highlight of the year. For Hannah, it was like being trapped in a family photo where everyone else was holding kids and she was the only one holding her breath.

And just when she thought she could fade into the background, Peninnah — her rival, her tormentor, her co-wife — would lean in across the food bowls with that saccharine smile and hiss, "God must really hate you." Right there. During grace. While everyone else was bowing their heads and saying *amen.* If Thanksgiving with your in-laws is rough, try adding animal blood on the altar and a rival whispering curses over your plate of roast lamb.

### Hannah's Life: A Play in Three Acts

### Act 1: The Annual Roast Session Every. Single. Year.

- Peninnah shows up looking like the Proverbs 31 woman

- Her kids are perfectly behaved (probably wearing matching outfits with bows and her hair is probably amazing. speculating. )
- Hannah's just sitting there like *"Can I get a refund on this marriage?"*

## Act 2: Elkanah's 'Comfort' That Makes It Worse

This poor man tries to help with: *"Am I not better to you than ten sons?"* (1 Sam 1:8) Translation: *"Babe, who needs kids when you've got... gestures vaguely at self"*

## Act 3: Hannah's Villain Origin Story Instead of:

- Poisoning Peninnah's fig cakes (tempting)
- Faking her own death (understandable)
- Running away from it all.

She does the unthinkable - she *goes to church* in full meltdown mode.

To be barren in such a holy place was to feel doubly forgotten — by people and by God. It is here Scripture uses the Hebrew phrase *marat nephesh* — "bitterness of soul." It was not just sadness. It was grief that hollowed a woman from within, a soul wrung dry like cloth twisted until it dripped everything.

## Why Hannah's Prayer Was Actually Genius

Hannah's prayer wasn't just heartfelt — it was downright genius. First of all, check her choice of location. She didn't pour out her soul in the kitchen, or in some quiet corner under a tree. No, she marched straight into the tabernacle, the very place where God's presence was said to dwell. It was bold, almost brazen. The modern equivalent would be like showing up uninvited at the White House, walking right past security, and ugly-crying in the Oval Office. If you're going to beg for a miracle, why not do it in the one place you're guaranteed to get Heaven's attention?

Then there was her method. Hannah prayed silently, lips moving but no sound coming out. This wasn't some serene yoga-class meditation moment — it was raw, wordless anguish. Her body shook, her face streaked with tears, and the only evidence of her prayer was the desperate movement of her mouth. It looked less like dignified devotion and more like someone falling apart in real time. Even the priest on duty, Eli, thought she was drunk. But what he mistook for wine-babbling was actually the soundless groaning of a woman who had run out of words and still refused to quit.

And then came the vow — the promise that shifted history. In the middle of her despair, Hannah made a deal with God: *"If you give me a son, I'll give him back to you."* In other words: *"Take the very thing I want most, the thing that defines my worth in this world, and make it Yours."* That wasn't bargaining; it was surrender on steroids. Who prays like that? Who asks for their greatest desire only to promise to hand it right back? Hannah did. Absolute madlad energy.

### When You Relate Too Hard:

You know those moments when you're scrolling Instagram, seeing everyone's perfect lives while you're eating cold pizza in a messy bun? Or when someone gives you that "comfort" that actually makes everything worse—like *"At least you have your health!"*—while you're faking being fine at church and secretly wanting to scream into the pew cushion? Your modern "Shiloh Feast" might be family gatherings where Aunt Karen bombards you with *"So when are you having kids? When will you get married? Have you found someone yet? What do you plan on doing with your future?"* It could be baby showers where you hide in the bathroom, weddings where you pray no aunties ask you to catch the bouquet, or those brutal Church Mother's Day services where they hand out flowers to all the moms while you sit there empty-handed, trying not to ugly-cry in the third row.

But Hannah teaches us That God hears us.

## Why Getting Mistaken for Drunk is a Spiritual Flex

When priest Eli accuses her of being wasted, Hannah drops the mic: *"I am a woman deeply troubled... pouring out my soul to the Lord."* (1 Sam 1:15)

### Breaking This Down:

- *"Pouring out"* = Hebrew "shaphak" - like tipping a jug completely upside down
- She wasn't holding back a single drop of her pain

Modern Translation: *"Sir, this isn't liquor - it's unresolved trauma."*

This was the turning point — a moment history would remember. Alone before God, Hannah wept silently, her lips moving though no sound escaped. She poured out her soul, promising that if God would look upon her misery and grant her a son, she would give him back to Him all his days. In the shadows of Shiloh, amidst the incense and silence, her anguish became offering.

And with those words, something shifted. Hannah rose, wiped her face, and returned to the feast. Scripture notes with quiet power: *"Her face was no longer downcast."* She still bore no child, yet the burden had been lifted. She had left her anguish at the altar and carried away peace — not ordinary peace, but the kind Paul later described: *"the peace of God, which surpasses all understanding, will guard your hearts and minds in Christ Jesus."* The kind of peace that makes no earthly sense, yet steadies the soul.

Centuries later, Jesus would invite the weary with words that echo Hannah's moment: *"Come to Me, all you who are weary and burdened, and I will give you rest... Take My yoke upon you and learn from Me, for I am gentle and humble in heart, and you will find rest for your souls."* Hannah had exchanged her yoke of sorrow for His yoke of rest. The cradle was still empty, but hope had been conceived in her heart.

## The Aftermath: Proof God Loves Hot Messes

### Immediate Peace

- She walks away with no baby bump
- **She returns to her husband and the woman trying to make her life more miserable.**
- But with inexplicable calm (Phil 4:7 vibes)

### Divine Turnaround

- Gets pregnant with Samuel ("God heard")
- Later has FIVE more kids (1 Sam 2:21)
- Peninnah's somewhere *seething*

**Legacy Beyond Herself**

- Samuel becomes the prophet who anoints King David which then leads to Jesus.. Yep, That messy prayer made it that far.
- Your messy prayers can impact generations

\*\*\*

**Your Hannah Prayer Playbook**

**Find Your Tabernacle**

- Your car? Shower? store parking lot? Toilet with a lock in it, so kids cant barge in.
- Where can you be *real* before God?

**Pour It ALL Out**

- Angry? Tell Him
- Jealous? Admit it
- Desperate? Scream it
- Don't Know? let him know

**Make Bold Promises**

- *"God if You ___, I'll ___"*

- Warning: He might take you up on it
- No Guarantee he will, but He will do something with it.

**Discussion Starters:**

1. What's your "Peninnah problem" right now?
2. Where's your modern "tabernacle" for raw prayers?
3. Try Hannah's silent prayer method today - what happens?

**Final Thought:** God isn't scared of your mess - He's waiting in it. So go ahead. Ugly cry. Bargain wildly. Change history.

*(Just maybe warn your priest or pastors, you're having a Hannah moment first.)*

# Chapter 6

# Hannah's Ugly Prayer

**O**R: **HOW A HOT MESS PRAYER SESSION CHANGED HISTORY**

> *"In her deep anguish Hannah prayed to the Lord, weeping bitterly. And she made a vow, saying, 'Lord Almighty, if You will only look on Your servant's misery and remember me, and not forget Your servant but give her a son, then I will give him to the Lord for all the days of his life...'"* — 1 Samuel 1:10–11

Hannah sank to her knees, pressing them into the packed earth floor. Her hands may have trembled against her skirt. The words of Scripture describe her as *marat nephesh* — "bitter of soul." This was no passing sadness; it was grief that consumed her identity. But then another word is used: she *shaphak* — poured out her soul before the Lord (1 Samuel 1:15). The image is of tipping over a jar until not a drop is left. Hannah emptied herself completely; no grievance, no tear, no hidden thought was withheld.

And then came her vow, perhaps the boldest part of all. She addressed God as *Yahweh Sabaoth* — "Lord of Hosts," Commander of heaven's armies. She dared to call on Him not as a distant deity but as a warrior God who could intervene in her battle. Her request was sharp in its simplicity: *"Look on Your servant's misery. Remember me. Do not forget me."* In Hebrew, *zakar* — "remember" — is not passive. It is active remembrance, covenant action. She was not begging God to think of her kindly. She was asking Him to act.

And her vow: *"If You give me a son, I will give him back to You all the days of his life."* In ancient Israel, vows were binding promises. To offer her longed-for child back to God as a Nazarite was unthinkable. No mother made such a vow lightly. But Hannah did — not to manipulate God, but to surrender. This was not a bargain but an offering. What she longed for most, she laid at His feet.

### The Prayer That Broke All the Rules

Let's freeze-frame Hannah's most iconic moment - when she marched into church looking like she'd just been dumped, cried so hard they thought she was drunk, and walked out with a miracle baking in her womb.

This wasn't just prayer - this was spiritual *performance art*. Let's break it down like we're watching game film of the most effective prayer in the Bible:

### Breaking Down The Prayer Move By Move
### 1. The Ugly Cry (1 Samuel 1:10)

- Hebrew phrase: *Marat Nephesh* - "bitterness of soul"

- Not just sad—*hollowed out* by grief
- Like when you cry so hard your face hurts the next day

## 2. The Pouring Out (1 Samuel 1:15)

- Hebrew word: *Shaphak* - to dump something out completely

  - Picture flipping over a water cooler until *glug glug glug* - nothing left
  - This was prayer with *no filter*

## 3. The Bold Ask (1 Samuel 1:11)

- Called God *Yahweh Sabaoth* - "Lord of Angel Armies"

  - Flex: She didn't beg the fertility gods like her neighbors would
  - Went straight to the Commander-in-Chief

## 4. The Crazy Vow

- "I'll give him back!"

  - Ancient Hebrew vows were *binding contracts*
  - Like signing over custody of your unborn child

## How God Responded to This Hot Mess Prayer

The way God responded to Hannah's "hot mess" prayer is almost as surprising as the prayer itself. First came peace — long before the miracle. When she rose from the tabernacle, Hannah was still barren. Nothing had changed on the outside. But Scripture says, *"Her face was no longer sad"* (1 Samuel 1:18). That wasn't because she suddenly had test results or baby names picked out. It was the kind of peace you get after you've ugly-cried in the shower — face blotchy, hair a mess, but somehow you feel lighter, steadier, like the weight isn't all on you anymore. What settled on her was exactly what Paul would later describe centuries later: *"the peace of God, which surpasses all understanding, will guard your hearts and your minds in Christ Jesus"* (Philippians 4:7). God hadn't given her the answer yet, but He had given her Himself.

Then came the miracle. In due time, Hannah conceived and gave birth to a son. She named him Samuel, which literally means *"God heard."* Because of course that's what you'd call him. Every time she said his name, it was like announcing to the world, "Yes — God listens. He heard me. He sees me." In a culture where names weren't just labels but declarations, Samuel's very existence was living proof that Hannah's whispered, wordless prayer had reached heaven.

And because God has a way of outdoing Himself, Samuel wasn't the end of the story. After she dedicated him to the Lord, Hannah went on to have five more children (1 Samuel 2:21). Five! It's as if God was saying, "Oh, you thought I was done? Sweetheart, that was just the beginning." The woman who once wept over an empty womb became the mother of a full house. Her hot mess prayer had not only opened the door to peace but unlocked an overflow of blessing she couldn't have scripted if she tried.

***

## Your Turn: Praying Like A Hannah

So, how do you pray like Hannah — the woman who walked into God's house, dumped her entire soul on the floor, and somehow walked out lighter? Let's break it down.

### 1. Find Your Tabernacle

Hannah went straight to the tabernacle, God's literal dwelling place. For us, that doesn't have to mean a church building. It just means finding *your* spot — the place where you can be brutally honest with God. Somewhere you don't care if your mascara runs, your voice cracks, or your nose makes noises. For me? It's the shower. The steam makes a surprisingly holy atmosphere, and it conveniently washes away tears and snot. Hannah's tabernacle might have been sacred stone; yours could be the driver's seat of your car, the laundry room, or that corner of your bed where you curl up when everything feels too heavy.

### 2. Pour Out Before You Ask

Notice Hannah didn't march in with a polished, three-point prayer list. She started by pouring out her soul. The Hebrew word *shaphak* literally means "to spill, to dump out." She emptied herself first — bitterness, anguish, shame, all of it — and *then* she made her request. That's a good order to follow. Cry if you need to. Name the pain before you name the solution. Ugly cry is not only allowed, it's sacred.

### 3. Dare the "Crazy" Vow

Here's the wild part. Hannah didn't just ask for a son — she vowed to give him back to God. That's not like promising to volunteer more at church if God fixes your finances. This was her greatest dream, the thing her entire identity and security depended on. And she basically said, "If You give me this, I'll surrender it right back." Heavy, right? Because if she hadn't followed through, it would've been catastrophic — spiritually, socially, even legally. Vows weren't casual in her culture; they were binding. Yet she kept it. She gave Samuel back. And God didn't just honor her vow — He multiplied her blessings.

So maybe we don't all make vows exactly like Hannah, but the principle stands: God honors surrendered dreams. Try it. Pray with that kind of reckless faith. Just... fair warning? He takes these seriously.

### When Your Prayer Gets Misunderstood...

Sometimes when you really pray — the messy, gut-level kind — people just won't get it. Hannah didn't exactly come off looking "spiritual." She looked drunk. Eli, the priest, literally told her to sober up. That's what happens when your prayer leaks raw emotion: someone will call you "too much," or tell you to calm down, or suggest you do it more properly, more politely. And then, to top it off, you might not see anything change right away. Hannah left the tabernacle still barren. No baby. No quick miracle.

But that's where the supernatural perspective kicks in. On the surface it was just a woman sobbing silently while a confused old priest frowned at her. But in heaven's view? It was the exact moment God leaned in closer. Angels were being dispatched. The future was being rewritten in real time. It looked ordinary, even embarrassing — but it was actually seismic.

## Your Turn: Praying Like A Hannah

So, how do you pray like Hannah — the woman who walked into God's house, dumped her entire soul on the floor, and somehow walked out lighter? Let's break it down.

### 1. Find Your Tabernacle

Hannah went straight to the tabernacle, God's literal dwelling place. For us, that doesn't have to mean a church building. It just means finding *your* spot — the place where you can be brutally honest with God. Somewhere you don't care if your mascara runs, your voice cracks, or your nose makes noises. For me? It's the shower. The steam makes a surprisingly holy atmosphere, and it conveniently washes away tears and snot. Hannah's tabernacle might have been sacred stone; yours could be the driver's seat of your car, the laundry room, or that corner of your bed where you curl up when everything feels too heavy.

### 2. Pour Out Before You Ask

Notice Hannah didn't march in with a polished, three-point prayer list. She started by pouring out her soul. The Hebrew word *shaphak* literally means "to spill, to dump out." She emptied herself first — bitterness, anguish, shame, all of it — and *then* she made her request. That's a good order to follow. Cry if you need to. Name the pain before you name the solution. Ugly cry is not only allowed, it's sacred.

### 3. Dare the "Crazy" Vow

Here's the wild part. Hannah didn't just ask for a son — she vowed to give him back to God. That's not like promising to volunteer more at church if God fixes your finances. This was her greatest dream, the thing her entire identity and security depended on. And she basically said, "If You give me this, I'll surrender it right back." Heavy, right? Because if she hadn't followed through, it would've been catastrophic — spiritually, socially, even legally. Vows weren't casual in her culture; they were binding. Yet she kept it. She gave Samuel back. And God didn't just honor her vow — He multiplied her blessings.

So maybe we don't all make vows exactly like Hannah, but the principle stands: God honors surrendered dreams. Try it. Pray with that kind of reckless faith. Just... fair warning? He takes these seriously.

## When Your Prayer Gets Misunderstood...

Sometimes when you really pray — the messy, gut-level kind — people just won't get it. Hannah didn't exactly come off looking "spiritual." She looked drunk. Eli, the priest, literally told her to sober up. That's what happens when your prayer leaks raw emotion: someone will call you "too much," or tell you to calm down, or suggest you do it more properly, more politely. And then, to top it off, you might not see anything change right away. Hannah left the tabernacle still barren. No baby. No quick miracle.

But that's where the supernatural perspective kicks in. On the surface it was just a woman sobbing silently while a confused old priest frowned at her. But in heaven's view? It was the exact moment God leaned in closer. Angels were being dispatched. The future was being rewritten in real time. It looked ordinary, even embarrassing — but it was actually seismic.

## Final Thought: Let's Get Real for a Minute

You know what I've learned from Hannah? Prayer isn't God's version of an American Idol audition. He's not Simon Cowell sitting on His heavenly throne critiquing our performance - "Hmm, interesting key choice on that worship song. Three stars." No ma'am.

Hannah taught me that prayer is more like...well, picture this: you know those ugly-cry face memes we all laugh at? That's basically what Hannah brought before God. Mascara running, snot bubbles, the whole package. And you know what's wild? That hot mess prayer session launched one of the greatest prophets in history.

Let me ask you something - when was the last time you really let loose in prayer? I'm not talking about those Pinterest-perfect "Father God, we just come before You" moments (though those have their place). I mean those raw, middle-of-the-night, "God if You don't show up I'm gonna lose it" kind of prayers. Those are the ones that seem to get heaven's attention.

And can we just acknowledge how ridiculous it is that we try to pretty things up for God? He literally knows every thought before we think it (Psalm 139:2), yet we're over here like, "Let me just edit this prayer real quick before I send it up." Girl, stop. The Creator of the universe isn't checking your spiritual grammar or making sure you quote three Bible verses before making your request.

Here's what I want you to try this week: pray one completely unfiltered prayer. Maybe it's:

- "God, I'm so angry about..."
- "I don't even believe You'll do this but..."
- *Silent screaming into a pillow while ugly crying*

And then watch what happens. Because here's the secret - the more real you get, the more room you give God to move. Hannah gave up pretending, and God gave her not just one miracle baby, but six kids total. Now that's what I call a holy plot twist.

So what's holding you back today? Fear of looking foolish? Newsflash - Hannah looked straight-up drunk to the priest. Worried your words aren't holy enough? Guess what - groans and tears are heavenly languages (Romans 8:26). Feeling like your situation is too messed up? Sweet friend, God specializes in impossible.

Your imperfect prayers are perfect to the One who sees your heart. So go ahead - let it all out. I'll be over here cheering you on (and maybe stealing some of your prayer ideas, because clearly they work).

*Now we've got some world-changing prayers to pray.*

# Chapter 7

# Lessons from Hannah's Prayer

**OR: HOW TO GET GOD'S ATTENTION WITHOUT FANCY WORDS**

*"Then Hannah prayed and said: 'My heart rejoices in the Lord; in the Lord my horn is lifted high. My mouth boasts over my enemies, for I delight in Your deliverance.'"* — 1 Samuel 2:1

### From Hot Mess To Heroic Faith

Let's be real—if we saw Hannah's story play out today, we'd call it a Lifetime movie plot:

- Bullied wife
- Drunk-crying in church
- Miracle baby
- Giving said baby away (WHAT?!)
- Ends up with six kids and probably no stretch marks

Hannah got an actual manual for effective prayer approved by God Himself. And lucky for you, I've reverse-engineered it like the Kingdom's worst kept secret.

## The "Why Was She So Extra?" Method (1 Samuel 1:10-11)

Remember how Hannah showed up at church looking like a train wreck?

Hannah didn't stroll into the tabernacle with her hair neatly braided and her prayer journal tucked under her arm. Scripture says she was *"deeply distressed and prayed to the Lord, weeping bitterly"* (1 Samuel 1:10). In other words, she showed up looking like a total train wreck. Picture it: red eyes, streaked mascara, ugly sobbing, lips moving with no sound coming out. Not exactly Sunday-best vibes.

To the people around her, it probably felt awkward — like she was barging into the pastor's office during Vacation Bible School, interrupting the craft station meltdown with, "Excuse me, I need to cry in God's face right now." But what looked "extra" to everyone else was exactly what got heaven's attention.

And here's why it worked: Hannah wasn't vague. She didn't pray some general "Bless me, Lord" prayer. She went full specificity. *"Lord Almighty, if You will only look on Your servant's misery and remember me, and not forget Your servant but give her a son, then I will give him to the Lord for all the days of his life"* (1 Samuel 1:11). That's not a polite, fill-in-the-blank kind of prayer. That's a laser-focused, no-holds-barred ask.

God responds to that kind of shameless specificity. It's the difference between saying, "Bless my finances" and "God, I need $1,382 to cover rent by Friday." Or swapping out, "Be with my kid" for, "Please, Lord, help Tiffany stop vaping behind the bleachers before the principal calls me again." Being extra in prayer isn't about drama — it's about daring to be precise. Hannah teaches us that desperation mixed with detail is powerful.

It's the same principle Jesus spelled out centuries later: *"Ask, and it will be given to you; seek, and you will find; knock, and the door will be opened to you"* (Matthew 7:7). Notice He didn't say, "Hint vaguely." He said ask. Knock. Be bold enough to press the doorbell until heaven answers. Hannah knocked until God swung the door wide open.

So go ahead. Bring your messy, specific, too-much prayers to God. He's not rolling His eyes. He's leaning

### The "No Take-Backsies" Prayer

Hannah didn't just *ask* for a baby—she signed a spiritual contract. In Bible terms, this was a Nazirite vow: no wine, no haircuts, just full-on dedication. Basically God's version of *"I'm serious—pinky swear."*

### How she followed through:

1. Got pregnant (obviously)
2. Survived toddler years (absolute hero)
3. Handed her kid to the same priest who'd accused her of being drunk (*next-level faith*)

**Pro Tip:** Only vow what you're ready to do. Ecclesiastes 5:5 basically says *"Don't play with God—He remembers your Venmo promises."*

After getting her miracle? Hannah threw down the mic with a prophetic worship song.

*Verse 1:*
"My mouth boasts over my enemies" (*Subliminal tweet at Peninnah*)
*Chorus:*
"The bows of warriors are broken" (*God's got my back now*)
*Bridge:*
"He raises the poor from the dust" (*That's MY testimony!*)

Her praise wasn't *for* the miracle—it bubbled up *from* the surrendered place. When God shows out for you:

- Do a kitchen dance like David (2 Samuel 6:22—look it up)
- Text your prayer squad the receipts
- Blast worship music in the shower like it's your personal Grammys

Hannah's story proves three game-changing truths:

God loves your mess Your chaotic, unedited prayers don't need a trigger warning. He prefers the raw director's cut over the sanitized Sunday school version.

Miracles love RSVPs The more specific your ask, the louder heaven's *"Say less fam"* response. None of this *"bless my finances"* vagueness—try *"I need $1,287 by Friday."*

## When God's "No" Is Really a "Just Wait Till You See This"

Let me tell you about the time God pulled a Hannah-level plot twist in my life. Picture this:

**Act 1:** Miracle pregnancy after grown kids! Cue the confetti, nursery Pinterest boards, and me ugly-crying in the OB's office like "GOD STILL DOES MIRACLES Y'ALL!" I was amazed, in awe, scared and sooo soo excited.

**Act 2:** Devastating miscarriage. Saddest day of my life . Me sobbing in hospital gown: *"But I wanted to mom RIGHT this time! No survival mode! Just snuggles and organic purees!"* I carried that pain for so long but got to the point of surrender. I would never exchange the feeling of carrying her for the few months I did.

**Act 3:** but Months of desperate prayers for another child that basically amounted to me being depressed and sad all the time which lead to true surrender: *"Fine. If I can't have a baby, flood my house with sticky-fingered chaos."* (Hannah-level negotiating right there)

I prayed and negotiated, I get it God, maybe this is not what you have instore for me. But fill my home with children I can pour out my love onto.

**Divine Plot Twist:** Within a YEAR:

- Daughter #1: Pregnant .. even she was surprised. . A Healthy amazing Huge Huge girl of 4.5 kg named Adeline. 1st child.
- Daughter #2: Surprise! Also pregnant . with her second girl Aiannah, chunky chipmunk
- Daughter-in-law: "can you pray for me, We're trying to... oh wait never mind, already pregnant" with her second boy who is all handsomeness .
- Bonus babies from friends falling like divine dominoes Not to mention our first boy grandchild and Ramona our girl who were already kicking around and eating all the treats in the cupboard.

God's response to my surrendered prayer wasn't what I expected—it was BETTER. He upgraded me from ma to *grandma*—the ultimate life hack where you get all the baby snuggles but hand them back when the diapers get nasty.

**What Hannah Knew That We Forget:**

**God specializes in holy bait-and-switch**

- You ask for A
- He gives you A+++ in a way you never imagined

**Surrender isn't defeat—it's strategy**

My white-knuckled grip on "must have baby" kept me from seeing the grandbaby avalanche coming. Surrendering became the best move, trusting that God just knows better and knows more than me. And he always has plans for me. And I can now with certainty know, that they are for Good and even when I may argue and think my plan is better, I can now readily release and surrender and trust his plan

Your "worst day" might be heaven's setup

That hospital grief became the fertilizer for my current "grandma era" and in that way, the memories and hope of our baby, now lives on each time i get a cuddle, each time i get a kiss from one of our sweet grandbabies. I still get to pour out that love to not just one child, but to many

## Your Turn: The Surrender Experiment

Try Hannah's (and my) playbook:

## Name Your "Samuel"
What's the thing you're white-knuckling? Write it down

## Pray The Scary Prayer

- *Surrender the pain of it*
- *Surrender it to God*
- *"God if not ___, then ___"*
- (Example: *"If not marriage, give me community that fills my cup"*)

## Surrender is the ultimate power move
When you stop white-knuckling your dreams, God starts showing off. Hannah didn't get *just* Samuel—she got five more kids and a legacy.

So go ahead—pray something so audacious it would make your small group clutch their pearls. And if anyone says you're *too much*?

Sweet friend, so was Hannah.

What's your "I wanted A but got B" story? Or I had to surrender story?

*"Now go make some holy noise. Now excuse me while I go sniff a newborn's head for spiritual inspiration."*

# MARY MOTHER OF JESUS

*"The angel went to her and said, 'Greetings, you who are highly favored! The Lord is with you.'"*
(Luke 1:28)

# Chapter 8

# The Story of Mary

***O**R: HOW A TEENAGE GIRL BECAME HISTORY'S MOST FAMOUS MOM*

> *"The angel went to her and said, 'Greetings, you who are highly favored! The Lord is with you.'"* (Luke 1:28)

Picture this with me: Nazareth, circa 4 BC. Not exactly the hotspot of the ancient world. More like...the armpit of Galilee. The kind of place where everyone knew everyone's business, where the smell of sheep dung mixed with baking bread, and where the local gossip traveled faster than a Roman messenger.

Our girl Mary was probably about 14—yes, you heard that right—fourteen. In our world, that's barely out of middle school, but in her time? Prime marriage material. She'd spent her childhood learning how to grind grain, carry water jars (without spilling! I can't carry a coffee 3 feet without a spill), and weave cloth like every other village girl. Her big dreams probably involved marrying Joseph the carpenter (solid guy, good with his hands), having a few kids, and living a quiet life where the biggest drama was whose goat got into whose garden.

Then BAM—Tuesday afternoon, she's probably kneading dough or sweeping the floor when suddenly her kitchen lights up like a TikTok filter gone wild. Enter Gabriel, heaven's top messenger angel, looking like he just stepped out of a Marvel movie.

"Greetings, favored one!" he says.

Now, let's pause here. When an angel calls you "favored," it's not like winning a free coffee. In Mary's world, God's favor often looked suspiciously like hardship waiting to happen. Just ask Moses (desert), David (caves), or Joseph (pit then prison). So Mary's first reaction? Absolute terror. The Bible says she was "deeply troubled"—which is Bible-speak for "she nearly peed her robes."

Gabriel continues: "You're gonna have God's baby. He'll be the Messiah."

Mary's brain short-circuits. On one hand: HOLY COW AN ANGEL. On the other: "But...I'm a virgin?" (Cue teenage awkwardness.) She's not doubting God—she's just confused about the mechanics. Like, "Um, does Joseph need to be involved in this plan or...?"

Meanwhile, back in Nazareth, the rumor mill is about to go into overdrive. In Mary's culture:

- Engagement was legally binding—breaking it required divorce papers

- Pregnancy before marriage = scandal of epic proportions
- The punishment? Could be anything from public shaming to stoning

Mary knows all this. Yet her response? "I am the Lord's servant. May it be done to me according to your word." (Luke 1:38)

Translation: "This makes zero sense, but okay God—let's do this."

## THE WALK OF SHAME (LITERALLY)

Fast-forward a few months. Mary may be showing now. Joseph—good man that he is—initially plans to divorce her quietly. But after his own angelic encounter, he sticks by her side.

Cue the Nazareth gossip train: -"Did you hear about Mary?" -"That's Joseph's girl, right? Pregnant before the wedding?" -"Claims it's 'God's baby'—sure, Jan."

Meanwhile, Caesar Augustus drops his census bombshell, forcing Joseph to trek 90 miles to Bethlehem. Mary—now VERY pregnant—has to go too.

Let me paint this journey:

- No comfy donkey rides like the Christmas cards show—more like hobbling alongside the animal
- Dusty roads, bandit risks, and zero roadside bathrooms
- Sleeping under the stars with a belly the size of a watermelon
- Keep away from the masses in fear of shame chatter

When they finally reach Bethlehem? Every AirBnB is booked. The innkeeper takes one look at sweaty, swollen Mary and is like, "Best I can do is the barn."

So the King of the universe enters the world:

- Not in a palace
- Not even a clean guest room
- But a cave-stable reeking of animals, with a feeding trough for a bassinet

Yet in this mess, Mary does something extraordinary—she treasures every moment. The shepherds' crazy story about angel karaoke? She "ponders it in her heart." The weird gifts from foreign wise men? She files that away too.

**WHY THIS MATTERS TO US**
Mary's story teaches us:

1. **God Uses Ordinary People**

Mary wasn't royalty. She wasn't famous. She was a nobody from nowhere—yet God chose her. Where you come from doesn't disqualify you.

2. **Obedience Often Looks Like Scandal**

Following God sometimes means looking foolish to others. Mary risked her reputation, her marriage, even her life.

3. **Grace Comes in Messy Packages**

The Messiah arrived covered in afterbirth, laid in animal feeding bowl. Your breakthrough might not look Instagram-perfect either.

**YOUR TURN: MARY'S PRAYER PLAYBOOK**

Mary's story shows us that prayer isn't just about words — it's about posture. Her life was one long "yes" to God, even when it made zero sense in the moment. So how do we pray like Mary? Let's walk through it together.

## Embrace the Unexpected

Mary was probably around fourteen, planning a quiet life with Joseph, maybe dreaming about bread recipes or a simple home. Then boom — an angel shows up with the ultimate curveball: *"You will conceive and give birth to a son, and you are to call him Jesus"* (Luke 1:31). Not exactly on her Pinterest board. But here's the thing: her response wasn't panic or bargaining. It was surrender. *"Let it be to me according to your word"* (Luke 1:38). That's a masterclass right there.

So the next time life flips your plans upside down, try Mary's move. Instead of spiraling, whisper: "God, is this You? Because if it is... help me say yes." That's not weakness. That's bravery wrapped in faith.

## Trust the Process

Mary didn't get a sneak peek at Easter Sunday when she laid Jesus in the manger. She couldn't see the resurrection from that stable — all she could see was a baby in swaddling clothes. Yet she trusted step by step, treasuring each moment, even when she didn't understand (Luke 2:19). That's hard for us, isn't it? We want the whole map before we take the first step. But faith, real faith, is walking when you can't see the finish line.

When you're stuck in the middle — the messy, waiting part — remember Proverbs 3:5–6: *"Trust in the Lord with all your heart and lean not on your own understanding; in all your ways submit to him, and he will make your paths straight."* Mary lived that verse before it was ever written down.

## Worship in the Mess

Let's not forget the setting. This wasn't a sanitized nativity scene with glowing halos and clean straw. This was a barn, crowded and noisy, probably smelling like every farmyard you've ever avoided. Yet right there, in the middle of the chaos, Mary cradled the Messiah and broke into song (Luke 1:46–55). Worship wasn't reserved for the temple; it erupted right there in the mess.

That's a reminder for us: you don't need the perfect atmosphere to meet God. You can worship Him in the hospital room, the kitchen sink, the backseat of your car, or in a season of total disorder. Isaiah 7:14 says, *"The virgin will conceive and give birth to a son, and will call him Immanuel"* — which means "God with us." With us... even in the chaos.

So here's the playbook: Embrace the unexpected. Trust the process. Worship in the mess. Mary's story shows us that prayer doesn't need to be polished. It just needs to be surrendered.

\*\*\*

## Discussion Time:

1. Where's your "Nazareth"—the thing people hold against you?
2. What's one thing God's asking you to trust Him with, even if it doesn't make sense?
3. How can you worship in your current "stable" situation?

Mary's "yes" changed history. Yours could too. So the next time God calls you to something scary, remember—He's not looking for perfect people. Just willing ones.

God still picks unlikely people. Your *yes* might change history too.

*Now excuse me while I go hug a teenager and eat some questionable cheese.*

# Chapter 9

# Mary's Magnificat

***O**R THE START OF SISTERHOOD ANTHEMS.*

> *"My soul glorifies the Lord and my spirit rejoices in God my Savior, for He has been mindful of the humble state of His servant. From now on all generations will call me blessed."* — Luke 1:46-48

**MARY'S MOMENT OF PRAISE**

Alright, friend, grab your coffee or tea because we're diving deep into what I like to call Mary's "sisterhood praise" moment—the Magnificat. Picture this: Mary, just your average teenage girl (seriously, like 14 or so), sits down in a cozy place, maybe in her parents' living room in Nazareth, and what spills forth is praise that echoes through history. She's basking in the reality of bearing the Son of God, and her response? One of the most beautiful songs of gratitude ever recorded—no pressure, right?

## THE URGENCY OF PRAISE: WHAT'S GOING ON HERE?

To understand Mary's Magnificat, we need to take a little journey back in time. This isn't just a casual shout-out to God; it's a revolutionary anthem. Mary's context is everything.

Remember Hannah? (Yes, we're doing the storytelling magic where past leads into present, folks, but making it less confusing than Star Wars.) Hannah was that heartbroken woman praying in the temple for a baby, her anguish so great people thought she was drunk. She finally had Samuel and dedicated him to the Lord.

Fast-forward a few generations—now we have Mary, a young woman who has been blessed with a baby but with a twist of divine fate. She's not just having any child; she's giving birth to the Savior of the world!

So what does Hannah's story have to do with Mary? Great question! Both women are caught in their respective societal norms—Hannah's job was to have babies because that's how women measured success, while Mary faced the scandal of a divine pregnancy that could land her in serious trouble and judgment. Yet both respond to their circumstances with outstanding faith and an overpowering sense of purpose.

Now, let's take a look at some of the rich, soulful lines of Mary's song because each one is dripping with meaning.

## "MY SOUL GLORIFIES THE LORD"

Right out of the gate, Mary's not saying, "I feel great and all." Nope, she's proclaiming that her soul—the deepest part of her being—is shouting glory to God. This isn't a casual "thank you" fluff; this is an invitation to the heavens to take a bow for respects. Glorifying the Lord wasn't just the religious thing to do; it's a powerful declaration of identity and purpose. It's like shouting to the world, "Hey! Look what God is doing through little ol' me!"

## "AND MY SPIRIT REJOICES IN GOD MY SAVIOR"

She's not just happy; she's rejoicing. As in "throw a little dance party in the living room" kind of rejoicing. And notice how she links her joy to God as Savior. You may wonder, does she mean *Savior* in the traditional sense right now, or is she foreshadowing? Oh, it's a combo of both! In that moment, she recognizes that God has not only chosen her, but is also up to something bigger than herself, something that will affect generations to come. Isn't that a sweet reminder? Your realities might not be perfect, but you're part of a bigger story.

## "FOR HE HAS BEEN MINDFUL OF THE HUMBLE STATE OF HIS SERVANT"

Let's unpack *mindful* and *humble* here because these are power words. Mary doesn't scoff or flaunt. She's saying, "I know I'm a nobody in the vast cosmos—just a girl from Nazareth—but God's looking at me." That's humility paired with life-altering truth. It's like when someone at a gathering says, "Wow, you're here?!" when you weren't expecting to stand out. When God sees you, He sees potential and purpose. Your insecurities don't disqualify you; if anything, they remind you of how powerful grace is.

## "FROM NOW ON ALL GENERATIONS WILL CALL ME BLESSED"

Roll up your sleeves, folks, because this is the big claim! Similar to Hannah how she said if you give me a child, I will give him back, Mary is here speaking over her life. And How true it is. Till this day we see Mary statues, and she is always remembered. She called it, Claimed and and God said yes.

## CULTURAL CONTEXT: WHAT'S THE GOSSIP LIKE?

In Mary's time, being pregnant out of wedlock was a BIG deal. We're talking about potential social ostracism, gossip, and downright abandonment. Not to mention, the pressure of a virgin birth? Those rumors would fly faster than a toddler in a candy store. Yet, despite the potential fallout, Mary is praising God—deeply aware of the gravity of her situation, but also entrusting her life story to God's capable hands.

Imagine the intensity of that moment: She's surrounded not only by friends but by the weight of her destiny. It's kind of like walking into a room full of gossipers and proclaiming your biggest secret—the pulse of her praise was undoubtedly fierce, fueled by a wild hope that everyone would see beyond her circumstances.

## WHAT ABOUT HANNAH? SIDE BY SIDE

So, how do Hannah and Mary's stories interconnect? Besides being badass women of faith, they both relied on direct conversations with God through praise. Hannah prayed fervently for her miracle, dedicating Samuel, and lo and behold, Mary, too, was brazenly ready to submit her child back to God, albeit in a radically different twist of fate. Hannah's response paved the way for motherhood, showcasing how women's prayers can unleash divine movements in ways they often don't see at first.

## A PEEK INTO THE HEART: WHAT MIGHT WE NOT UNDERSTAND?

Just like any complex story, there's always more under the surface! Mary's praise goes beyond her personal experience; she's invoking a legacy of faith. She's tapping into the promises made to the people of Israel, reminding them that God's intention has always been to uplift the humble and empower the powerless.

Think about the days leading up to Mary's song; she's been through a whirlwind: angelic messages, confusion, societal judgment looming—a classic case of overwhelm. Her praise is akin to a double espresso shot of faith, reminding us that vulnerability does not equal weakness, but rather a fierce stance against life's pressures.

Let's inject a little humor here, because who doesn't love a snicker amidst the solemnity of faith? This girl Mary probably had her "what am I doing?" moments too. I mean, under all that spiritual weight, she was also the one who might have nervously chuckled at the idea of telling her friends about the angel visitation. "Yeah, you know, just hangin' out and having tea with Gabriel, NBD."

And here's a nugget of truth: *it's okay to laugh and find joy even when life is a rollercoaster.* Faith isn't all heavy burdens; sometimes it's a joyful dance in the face of craziness—like a joyful toddler engaging in the noodle dance (you know, the flopping around, joyous thing?)

Mary's praise doesn't just celebrate what God has done; it's a prophecy of what He will do. It's almost like she's channeling her inner parent: "When you grow up, you'll learn about all these moments, trust me!" Her song is rooted in the understanding that God's promises extend far beyond individual experiences into corporate blessings, affecting generations.

### FINALLY, WHY SHOULD MARY'S PRAISE MATTER TO US?

So, here's the heart-tether of the whole scenario: Mary's Magnificat is a clarion call for all of us—young or old, single or married, full of faith or silently skeptical. This prayer isn't just for her; it's a guide and a shout of encouragement for everyone, reminding us that God listens, acts, and responds—even when our lives feel messy.

When life gets overwhelming and you find yourself in a journey where the odds seem stacked against you, remember Mary's song. Recite it, sing it, meditate on it—allow it to wash over you. Praise, my friend, is powerful. And amidst the chaos, it can be your lifeline back to divine connection.

**Your Turn:** Connecting with Mary's Song

**Honor Your Vulnerability:** Next time you're feeling small or misunderstood, try expressing gratitude or praise—not just for what's good, but for the strength to endure the hard stuff.

**Celebrate Growth:** Think of a time you emerged from a tough situation—what would your *Magnificat* look like for that moment? Get creative!

**Engage in Humor:** Do you have a Mary-like "what am I doing?" story? Share it, laugh about it! Because faith doesn't have to be just piety; it can be pure joy amidst life's awkwardness.

So, there you have it. Mary's Magnificat isn't just a song; it's an anthem for anyone daring enough to believe in a bigger future! Now let's grab some tissues, or maybe cupcakes, because that's the kind of sustenance we need to celebrate divine moments in our lives.

# Chapter 10

# Lessons from Mary's Prayer

**OR: HOW A TEENAGE "YES" CAN STILL SHAKE THE WORLD**

*(Cue the angelic choir and maybe some faint goat noises from the stable because this chapter is about to hit you right in the spiritual feels.)*

Mary teaches us that the bravest prayers aren't the polished ones—they're the reckless "yeses" whispered through shaking lips when nothing makes sense.

God Chooses the Unqualified (Because He Specializes in Plot Twists)

Mary was:

- A *nobody* from *nowhere* (Nazareth = ancient Israel's version of the town you forget exists).

- Young, poor, and probably still trying to figure out how to braid her hair without getting it caught in her headscarf.
- Engaged, but definitely *not* planning on divine plot twists like virgin births.

Yet God didn't scroll through heaven's LinkedIn for "Most Impressive Candidate." He picked the girl who simply said, *"Let it be."* (Luke 1:38, Taylor's "Terrified But Willing" Translation).

Your inexperience, age, or social media following don't disqualify you. God works best through blank slates—less résumé, more availability.

Obedience Looks Like Scandal (And That's Okay)

Mary's obedience meant:

- Risking her marriage (*"Uh, Joseph, long story..."*)
- Facing societal shame (*"Blessed virgin? Sure, Mary."*)
- Literally birthing God in a barn (*"5-star Bethlehem accommodations right here."*)

Yet Jesus didn't arrive in palace-sanctioned splendor. He came through *scandal, whispers, and stable stench*—proof that God's plans don't cater to human approval ratings.

If your "yes" to God makes your conservative aunt clutch her pearls or your Instagram followers side-eye you... you're in good company.

***

Praise Is the Ultimate Power Move.

Mary's Magnificat (Luke 1:46–55) wasn't just gratitude—it was a theological grenade:

- *"He has brought down rulers but lifted up the humble."*
- *"The hungry filled with good things, the rich sent away empty."*

This wasn't a gentle lullaby. It was a *revolutionary anthem*. She praised God not just for *what He did for her*—but for *who He is*—a God who flips systems, shames pride, and elevates the overlooked.

Real praise isn't just for blessings—it's for *His character*, especially when life feels unstable.

Just like Mary, we're called to trust God's wild assignments—even when they don't come with a 5-year plan, a savings account, or society's stamp of approval.


Let me tell you about the time I tried to argue with God like a spiritual Karen.
Not even close to a Mary Level yes, but it was scary for me. The judgment, what would people say, I have never done this in public before and lay it all down for public scrutiny.

When I felt Him nudge me to *write this book*—the one you're holding. My response?
*"Uh, no. I'm:

- Not a theologian (*I Googled 'how to pray' last week*)
- Too busy (*see: 9 kids, 5 grandkids, 3 nervous breakdowns*)

- Absolutely terrified (*what if my pastor reads this and realizes I don't know Greek? What if i say something wrong?* )"\*

But then I remembered Mary. A *child* said yes to raising *God incarnate*, and I'm over here sweating a book deadline?

So I whispered (*through gritted teeth*), "Fine. If You're sure... just... help me please."

And guess what? *This*—right here—is me, still mid-process, proving that He doesn't need perfect obedience. Just willing surrender. (*Also, I sound so confident, but I'm literally only 2 women in, who knows when i will finish writing this, but you know, let God be God and do what he do.*)

## The Prayer Practice (How to "Mary" Your Life)

Mary's secret wasn't that she had it all figured out — it's that she dared to pray a scary *yes*. When the angel dropped the news, she could've said, "This makes no sense," or, "What if I fail?" Instead, she leaned into trust: *"May it be to me as you have said"* (Luke 1:38). That's gutsy faith.

So here's the challenge: what's the one thing God's nudging you toward that makes your stomach flip? Write it down. Name it. And then, even if your voice shakes, pray Mary's words over it: "Let it be to me according to Your word." You don't have to understand the whole plan. You just have to be willing to say yes.

And then there's the worship piece. Mary didn't wait until the angels sang, or the magi showed up with gold, or the story had a happy ending. She praised right there in the middle of her chaos — in what was basically a barn. She sang about God's mercy, His justice, His ability to lift the humble and fill the hungry (Luke 1:46–55). She worshiped before she saw a single promise fulfilled.

That's a prayer practice worth copying. Next time life feels like a mess — diapers on the floor, bills piling up, heart weighed down — try whispering: "God, I don't see the plan, but I see You." Swap out the complaints for Mary-style declarations: instead of, "I'm overwhelmed," pray, "You lift the humble." Instead of, "This is so unfair," pray, "You fill the hungry."

Mary teaches us that the prayer of surrender and the prayer of praise belong together. Say the scary yes, then sing the stubborn hallelujah. That's how you "Mary" your life.

Sweet friend, if you take anything from Mary's story, let it be this: God isn't waiting for you to have it all together. He's waiting for you to say *together*.

- Your shaky *"yes"* is enough.
- Your confused *"how?"* doesn't scare Him.
- And your messy prayers (*"God, are You sure about this??"*) still move heaven.

So go ahead—pray like a girl who just changed history. Because you might.

*(P.S. If you see me ugly-crying in the Target parking lot later, mind your business. Some of us are busy saying "yes.")*

# DEBORAH

*"Now Deborah, a prophet, the wife of Lappidoth, was leading Israel at that time. She held court under the Palm of Deborah between Ramah and Bethel in the hill country of Ephraim, and the Israelites went up to her to settle their disputes."*
— Judges 4:4-5 (NIV)

# Chapter 11

# The Story of Deborah

## OR: HOW A PROPHETESS IN COMBAT BOOTS BROKE EVERY RULE

*"Now Deborah, a prophet, the wife of Lappidoth, was leading Israel at that time. She held court under the Palm of Deborah between Ramah and Bethel in the hill country of Ephraim, and the Israelites went up to her to settle their disputes."* — Judges 4:4-5 (NIV)

### Welcome to Deborah's World (AKA Ancient Israel's Wild West Era)

So there I was, listening to this incredible story about ancient Israel around 1200 BC, and let me tell you, it was absolute chaos. There wasn't a king ruling over Israel at this time, which meant no central authority keeping everyone in line—just pure, relentless mayhem with different tribes doing whatever they thought was right. You can imagine how well that worked out.

Militarily speaking, things were looking pretty grim for the Israelites. They were getting completely dominated by King Jabin of Canaan and his general Sisera, who honestly sounds like he could have been a villain straight out of some epic drama. The Israelites were basically getting steamrolled at every turn.

And spiritually? Well, that's where things get really interesting. The people were spiritually weak, constantly rebelling against God, and desperately crying out for leadership that wouldn't march them straight into disaster. It was like watching a nation stuck in this endless cycle of "Can someone please step up who actually knows what they're doing?"

And in the middle of this dumpster fire? A woman named Deborah.

Not just any woman—**a prophetess, a judge, a military strategist, and a poet.** Basically, if Beyoncé and Ruth Bader Ginsburg had a baby in ancient Israel, it would be Deborah.

### DAILY LIFE OF A BIBLICAL BADASS

What did Deborah's average Tuesday look like? Let's sketch it out with historical accuracy (and a sprinkle of sass).

### Morning Routine

- Wakes up at dawn (no snooze button).
- Says her prayers (probably something like, *"God, please don't let Israel be Israel today"*).

- Combs her hair (because even warrior women deserve good hair days).

## Work Schedule

Judicial duties under her palm tree office (ancient Israel's version of an open-air courthouse).

Military briefings with local commanders (*"Sir, the Canaanites are charging—should we panic?"*).

Prophetic downloads (God whispering battle plans like a divine GPS).

Probably fighting every mans opinion of her, whenever she disagreed with them.

## Cultural Norms She Shattered

Listen, girl wasn't just holding down *a* leadership position—she was literally running the whole show. Picture this: while all the dudes are out here thinking they own politics and warfare, Deborah's basically operating as Israel's Supreme Court Chief Justice, five-star general, AND national prophet all wrapped up in one absolutely unstoppable package.

And honey, it wasn't like people were just politely asking her opinion and then doing whatever they wanted anyway—oh no. When Deborah spoke, generals actually listened and followed orders. Like, these big tough military guys were taking direct commands from her without question.

But here's where it gets really spicy—she wasn't content to just sit around giving prophetic fortune cookie messages. Nope. She was out there making sure God's verdicts actually happened on the battlefield. Talk about a woman who backed up her words with action!

## Fashion & Vibe Check

No flowing princess robes here. Deborah dressed for business—think sturdy tunics, maybe even some early version of combat boots (okay, sandals, but *serious* sandals).

Her *"Palm of Deborah"* wasn't just a chill picnic spot—it was where justice was served with zero tolerance for nonsense.

## Women Didn't Rule Like This

Sure, Israel had priestesses and wise women, but honey, none were out here commanding entire military operations.

Even in pagan cultures where goddess worship was a thing, warfare was still a testosterone-heavy boys' club—until God looked around and said, *"You know what? Let me send in Deborah to show these fellas how it's done."*

She Was Married too—But No "Stand by Your Man" Nonsense

Scripture mentions she's *"the wife of Lappidoth"* (Judges 4:4), but after that? Radio silence on hubby.

Some biblical scholars think *"Lappidoth"* literally means *"torches"*—so either she was married to a guy whose job was lighting things, or it's a fancy way of saying she was *the woman who brought the fire* while her husband stayed home doing... whatever husbands did when their wives were busy saving nations.

She Set Up Shop Under a Tree (Talk About Unconventional Office Space)

While Huldah the prophetess (2 Kings 22) worked the traditional temple circuit, Deborah said, *"Nah, I'll take my meetings outside under this palm tree, thanks."*

Her leadership style was completely accessible—no gatekeepers, no appointment systems, just show up and get some divine justice served with your morning coffee.

## She Didn't Just Prophesy—She Made It Happen

Most prophets were like spiritual news anchors: *"Thus saith the Lord, this is what's going down."*

Deborah? She was more like a spiritual military commander: *"Thus saith the Lord—and Barak, quit standing there with your mouth open, we've got a war to win!"*

Israel's crisis in Deborah's time? Brutal oppression under King Jabin of Canaan.

- 900 iron chariots (the ancient equivalent of tanks)
- 20 years of Israeli farmers forced into hiding (no crops = no food = no hope)
- Spiritual lethargy – Israel had forgotten God, so God *"sold them into the hands of Jabin"* (Judges 4:2)

Enter Deborah.

Her Burden: Watching her people suffer under tyranny.

Her Assignment: Deliver Israel—*without an army.*

**THE HIDDEN MEANING OF DEBORAH'S NAME**

**"Deborah" (דְּבוֹרָה) = "Bee"**
Bees are organized, fiercely protective, and produce sweet stuff (justice + prophetic words, in her case).
*Biblically*, bees symbolize **unstoppable divine order** (Psalm 118:12).

**"Lappidoth" (לְפִּידוֹת) = "Torches" or "Flashes of Fire"**
Some rabbis suggest her husband was named *Barak* ("lightning"), making their marriage a divine power couple (but that's a theory).
Others believe *"Eshet Lappidoth"* means "Woman of Torches"—a title of fiery leadership.
Either way, Deborah was lit—literally and spiritually.

**The Day Deborah Dropped the Mic on Israel's Top General (Judges 4:6-9)**

Alright, buckle up, because this moment is *peak Deborah*—equal parts divine strategy and holy sass. Picture it:

Deborah's sitting under her famous palm tree (because *obviously* a woman who hears from God directly doesn't need a stuffy throne room), probably sipping mint tea and reviewing Israel's latest disaster headlines. *"Canaanites rampaging... AGAIN. Farmers hiding in caves... STILL. Men refusing to lead... SHOCKING."*

Then *BAM*—God drops a mission in her spirit: *"Call Barak. Tell him it's go-time."*

Now, Barak wasn't just *some guy*. He was the military brass of Naphtali, a seasoned commander with—one assumes—impressive biceps and a sword collection.

But when Deborah summons him and delivers heaven's battle plan (*"Gather 10,000 troops, march to Mount Tabor, and watch Me hand Sisera's chariots over to you"* — Judges 4:6-7), his response is...

*"Uh... yeah, about that... I'll only go if YOU come with me."* (Judges 4:8, *Passive-Aggressive General Translation*).

Let's pause here.

Barak's Not Chicken—He's Human

This isn't cowardice; it's *imposter syndrome* on steroids. The man's facing 900 iron chariots (think: ancient tanks) with a militia of farmers carrying pitchforks. Of *course* he wants the living, breathing proof of God's presence (Deborah) by his side.

Bonus Hebrew nugget: Barak's name (בָּרָק) means *"lightning"*—yet here he is, hesitating like a teen asked to parallel park for the first time.

Deborah's Clapback is Legendary

She doesn't scold him. Doesn't sigh theatrically. Just fires back with: *"Fine, I'll go. But spoiler alert—the honor won't be yours. God's handing Sisera to a WOMAN."* (Judges 4:9, *Taylor's "Read the Room" Version*).

Fast-forward: Barak rallies the troops, they march out, and God drowns Sisera's chariots in a flash flood (Judges 4:15).

Sisera bails on foot—right into the tent of Jael, another woman who *"welcomes"* him with a tent peg to the skull (Judges 4:21).

Deborah's prophecy? 100% fulfilled. The villain's taken out not by the general, but by a housewife with a hammer.

### SO WHAT'S THE TAKEAWAY?

Here's the thing about Deborah's story: God seems to have a habit of using the hesitant, the overlooked, and the "are-you-sure-about-this-one?" types. Moses tried to talk his way out of leadership because of a stutter (Exodus 4:10). Gideon was literally hiding in a winepress when the angel called him a "mighty warrior" (Judges 6:11–12). Peter swore up and down he didn't even know Jesus — three times (Luke 22:54–62). And Barak? Let's be honest, he wouldn't go into battle without Deborah at his side. The guy basically needed a babysitter with a prophetic gift.

And yet — victory still came. Because God doesn't choose based on résumés, confidence levels, or cultural approval ratings. In this story, women get the last laugh. Twice. First Deborah, who leads Israel with wisdom and courage under her palm tree. And then Jael, the homemaker with a hammer, who takes down the enemy commander in her own tent. Coincidence? Not a chance. This was divine strategy.

Victory doesn't care about credentials. Deborah wasn't a trained soldier. Jael wasn't a professional assassin. But God handpicked them to change the course of history. That's why Deborah's palm tree honestly deserves a spot on Israel's version of Mount Rushmore. Forget stone faces of kings — give me a carved palm tree with Jael's tent peg next to it. That's the monument God delights in.

So if you've ever been told, "You don't belong in leadership because of your gender" — remember Deborah. She didn't need a throne, a crown, or even a sword. She had a palm tree, a prophecy, and the unshakable conviction that when God speaks, you stand up and act. And that was more than enough to rewrite Israel's story.

*(Now go be the Deborah in your own chaotic world. And might I suggest investing in a good pair of combat boots?)*

# Chapter 12

# Deborah's Song of Victory

## OR: HOW A PROPHETESS DROPPED THE MIC ON CANAAN'S ARMY

*"Then Deborah and Barak the son of Abinoam sang on that day..."* — Judges 5:1

### Israel's 20-Year Train Wreck

Okay, let's set the stage, because Deborah doesn't bust out her Grammy-worthy prayer until *after* the battle is won—but oh, the *drama* leading up to it. For twenty years, Israel was stuck in a toxic relationship with King Jabin of Canaan and his terror of a general, Sisera.

And in the middle of this mess? Deborah. Not waiting for permission. Holding court under a palm tree, taking names and processing complaints like Israel's most no-nonsense small claims judge.

Then one day—*BOOM*—God tells her: *"Enough. Call Barak. We're ending this."*

But remember how that went down? Barak, the supposed tough-guy general, basically whimpers, *"I'll only go if you come with me."* (Judges 4:8). Deborah, already over the spinelessness of men, sighs and says, *"Fine, but FYI, God's giving the trophy to a woman—not you."*

**Spoiler:** She was right. The real MVP? Jael, a housewife-turned-heroine who'd drive a tent peg through Sisera's skull later that day.

## The Prayer Itself: Part Prophecy, Part Victory Shout - A Song

Okay, first off, let's clear this up: Deborah's "prayer" wasn't a sweet, quiet, hands-folded, eyes-closed, whisper-to-Jesus kind of moment. Nope. Judges 5 is a full-blown victory anthem. Think less "silent meditation," more Beyoncé halftime show — only with prophetic lyrics and zero auto-tune. It's worship, war cry, history lesson, and rebuke all rolled into one.

You've got to read the whole thing in Judges 5 to get the flavor, but here's the play-by-play.

## She Starts with Praise (Because Worship is a Weapon)

Her opening line sets the tone: *"Bless the Lord! The leaders led in Israel, the people volunteered—praise the Lord!"* (Judges 5:2). She doesn't say, "Look what I did," even though she totally could've.

She doesn't take credit as the judge who rallied a scared general or as the prophetess who called the shots.

Instead, she points everyone's eyes upward. This wasn't Deborah's victory — it was God flexing His muscles through ordinary people. Context matters here: Israel had been bullied and oppressed for twenty years. They didn't even have weapons (Judges 5:8 says they had "not a shield or spear among forty thousand"). So when she shouts, "Praise the Lord!" it's not just hype — it's testimony.

### She Calls Out the Fakers

And then Deborah does what most church folks today are too polite to do: she straight up names names. Reuben? *"You sat in your fancy tents debating!"* (Judges 5:15–16). Translation: y'all had a committee meeting about maybe showing up, and while you were still arguing pros and cons, the battle was already won. Gilead? *"You stayed beyond the Jordan."* (v. 17). Basically, thanks for nothing. And Meroz? Oh, she doesn't just call them lazy — she pronounces a curse (v. 23). That's Bible talk for "you're canceled." The modern version would be like someone standing up at church after a community project and saying, "Yeah, so shoutout to those who showed up, and to those who ghosted us? May God handle you." Spicy.

### She Celebrates the Unexpected Heroes

And then — the highlight reel. She goes wild celebrating Jael: *"Most blessed of women is Jael!"* (Judges 5:24). Remember, Jael wasn't a warrior, she was a tent-dwelling housewife who knew her way around a mallet. While the men were hiding, she drove a tent peg straight through the skull of Sisera, the enemy commander. Savage. And here's a little Easter egg you might miss: that phrase "most blessed of women"? It shows up again centuries later about Mary, the mother of Jesus (Luke 1:28, 42). Two women, worlds apart, both called "most blessed." One crushed an enemy's head, the other carried the child who would crush the serpent's head. Coincidence? Nah, that's biblical poetry.

## She Ends with a Prophetic Mic Drop

Finally, Deborah closes her song with this zinger: *"So may all your enemies perish, Lord! But may those who love you rise like the sun in its strength."* (Judges 5:31). Translation: here's the scoreboard. God's enemies lose, God's friends shine. Pick a side. It's part prayer, part prophecy, part holy taunt — and it leaves no wiggle room.

So Deborah's "prayer" wasn't just thanks for a battle. It was a cultural reset, a history-making soundtrack. She wanted every ear in Israel (and every heart for generations) to know: God wins through unlikely people. Leaders who step up. Volunteers who show up. Women with tent pegs. Moms with prophecies.

If you've ever wondered whether your little "yes" to God matters, just remember Deborah's song. It was sung under a palm tree thousands of years ago, and we're still talking about it today.

## She Was *Fed Up* with Half-Hearted Faith

Deborah wasn't about to let anyone sit on the spiritual sidelines when God was moving. Her song reads like a divine attendance sheet—she called out tribes by name for their excuses while celebrating those who actually showed up. No diplomatic language, no gentle nudging. Just brutal honesty about who had

God's back when it mattered. This woman understood that lukewarm faith gets you lukewarm results, and she wasn't having any of it.

### She Saw God as a *Warrior*—Not Just a Gentle Shepherd

While other prayers focus on God's comfort and peace, Deborah's song is basically a war chant celebrating divine military strategy. She's out here praising God for drowning enemy chariots and routing armies like some kind of ancient cheerleader for heavenly warfare. This wasn't quiet, contemplative worship—this was full-throated celebration of God's power to absolutely demolish His enemies. She understood that sometimes love looks like justice, and justice sometimes looks like tent pegs to the skull.

### She Refused to Let Men Take Credit

Even though Barak got his moment in the victory song, Deborah made sure everyone knew the real MVP was Jael—the housewife who finished what the generals started. She deliberately highlighted how God used women to accomplish what the military couldn't, making it crystal clear that heaven's power doesn't follow earthly hierarchies. Her praise became a proclamation that God's kingdom operates by completely different rules than human expectations.

### How Others Misunderstood Her

- The Tribe Leaders: *"Why's she in charge?"* (Meanwhile, they're hiding in their basements.)
- The Culture: Expected women to be silent. Deborah sang louder.

- Even Future Theologians: Some tried to downplay her role. But God put her story in *Scripture*—twice.

## God's Response: 40 Years of Peace (Judges 5:31)

- No more oppression.
- No more chariots terrorizing farmers.
- **Just *peace*—because one woman dared to praise God publicly, call out cowards, and credit Him alone.

## Why This Matters for Us

Look, Deborah's prayer wasn't just some ancient one-hit wonder—it's basically your survival guide for when life gets messy. Think of it as your bestie handing you the playbook for celebrating God's victories even when you're still ugly-crying from trauma, calling out the people who ghosted you when things got tough (not to be petty, but to wake them up), and giving major props to the unexpected heroes God used to save the day. It's like she knew we'd need permission to praise loudly, point out problems honestly, and champion the underdogs who actually showed up.

*(Now go blast some victory music. Or, you know, a hammer clanging. Whatever works.)*

# Chapter 13

# Lessons from Deborah's Prayer

## "DEBORAH'S HANDBOOK TO BEING EXTRA: HOW TO PRAY LIKE YOU'RE THE HERO OF THE STORY (BECAUSE YOU ARE)"

*"Wake up, wake up, Deborah! Wake up, wake up, break out in song!"* - Judges 5:12 (NIV, but with some serious girl power energy)

Deborah teaches us that real prayer isn't about polite whispers - it's about bold declarations mixed with divine sass and fierce celebration.

### God Wants Your Whole Soundtrack, Not Just the Worship Songs

Remember when Deborah drops the mic with her victory song (Judges 5)? She doesn't just say "thank you Jesus" and call it a day. This woman serves us:

- Praise ("Bless the Lord!" v2)
- Roasts ("Why did Dan stay with the ships?" v17 - ouch)
- Historical bullet points ("In the days of Shamgar..." v6)
- Straight-up trash talk ("May all your enemies perish" v31)

She treats prayer like a Spotify worship playlist where every genre belongs. Your prayers can be this real too. God can handle your complaints with your confessions, your tears with your triumph.

*Fun Biblical Nugget:* The Hebrew word for her "song" (shir) is the same used for both battle cries and love songs. Talk about range!

### Don't Just Pray - Document That Stuff

Deborah's prayer isn't just spontaneous praise - it's a detailed record of:

- Who showed up (shoutout to Ephraim and Benjamin)
- Who flaked (looking at you, Reuben)
- Divine intervention (flash floods FTW)
- And who got wrecked (RIP Sisera)

This isn't coincidence - she's showing Israel how to remember God's faithfulness.

*Try This:* Next answered prayer, do a Deborah - write it down dramatically. "On this day, July 17th, when Starbucks forgot my coffee order BUT THE LORD PROVIDED A FREE REFILL..."

### Your Prayer Should Make Comfortable People Uncomfortable

Deborah's prayer isn't a gentle nudge - it names names ("Oh Meroz...cursed!" v23). She's calling out the spiritually lazy while celebrating the courageous (Jael MVP!).

Sometimes prayer isn't just asking God to move - it's calling out what's blocking His move in your life or community.

## Personal Tie-In (When I Tried to Deborah and Failed Spectacularly)

Lemme tell you about my first attempt at "Boldness Moment." I new in Christ, excited, finally pastor asks a question and gets the church involved in his sermon, and he is like who has a testimony. To be honest, sitting here thinking about it, i honestly can not even remember what my supposed testimony was going to be.. Well..Because of what came next.

See a few days prior all my washing got stolen off the line (that kind of neighborhood) but people came together and gave me clothes. See i had just moved in and washed absolutely everything. And God thought it be hilarious to let someone steal all my clothes.

Anyway, I had moved on, got some clothes from friends and some didn't fit quite right. So here I am in church, standing up to share a testimony or prayer request or something, when my pants fall down. Revealing the most amazing boy pants underwear. I sat down real quick, everyone had a laugh and I never shared my testimony.

But here's the thing - Deborah would've laughed it off and kept going. Because imperfect boldness > perfect silence every time.

What i have learnt since that time is to embrace the messy and the chaos, God has a plan and if i can just keep my eyes and focus on him then the rest is not as scary as it might seem. I don't seem to overthink or over fixate, i just let God be God.

## The Prayer Practice (How to Deborah Your Life)

### 1.  Turn Your Complaints Into Chants

Instead of just venting about what's wrong, write it down as a victory song-in-progress. Example: *"There was a day my WiFi failed me... BUT THEN THE LORD PROVIDED MOBILE DATA!"* Ok not the best example, but you get the concept. declaring God's win, is about faith, knowing that God is working this situation, knowing that God has a plan, knowing that God has already prepared a way, is what we celebrate.

### 2.  Start a Prayer Hall of Fame

Keep a "Deborah List" in your notes app recording:

- Who showed up for you (text them and say so!)
- What God did (be specific)
- What still needs conquering (future victory material)

If you haven't noticed, God has put an entire bible together spanning centuries of history. He really is in to writing things down. Record it. Sometimes we need to do the same with our own lives. See our minds can forget, can remember things incorrectly, put glory in the wrong places and mislead us, but writing it down and making it plain (Habakkuk 2:2), allows us to revisit and see God's work in our lives. .

### 3. **Pray With Your Whole Personality**

Fiery like Deborah? Pray loud. More introverted? Write it. Cry-er? Sob freely. God didn't give us personality tests - He gave us permission to come as we are. (Matthew 11:28)

I truly love that. I am often reminded of when the disciples came back to Jesus after being sent out. They came back exhausted, chased away, abused, angry some of them, but yet Jesus didn't turn away from them, when they came back explaining what had happened. He literally sat there and listened. He heard them all.

\*\*\*

## Encouragement / Blessing

Listen, spiritual queen — if God could use an outspoken woman in a world where women were supposed to be silent and invisible, He can absolutely use your "too much"-ness too. Deborah didn't tone it down, and neither should you.

Your prayers don't have to sound like the polished ones you hear at church, with carefully measured words and a soft "amen" at the end. If your prayers come out messy, emotional, or raw enough to make people squirm a little — perfect. That means they're real. God doesn't need rehearsed speeches; He wants your whole heart.

Deborah showed us that sometimes a prayer isn't even finished until it makes someone clutch their pearls and whisper, "She said *what* now?"

That's when you know you've stepped into the holy ground of bold honesty. So pray like the main character — because in God's story, you are. You were written into His narrative on purpose, with a voice that carries weight and a heart that He delights to hear from.

And hey — while Jael's tent peg moment makes a legendary sermon illustration, let's be clear: we're not endorsing hardware-store warfare. Leave the hammers in the shed. Your weapons are sharper: prayer, praise, and that stubborn kind of faith that refuses to back down.

So here's your blessing: May your voice rise like Deborah's under the palm tree, steady and fearless. May your prayers echo like songs of victory, even before the battle's won. And may your courage remind the world that God doesn't just call the qualified — He qualifies the called. Go forth, pearl-clutching honesty and all.

*"Let the righteous be glad... Let them sing for joy on their beds. Let the high praises of God be in their mouths, and a two-edged sword in their hand."* - Psalm 149:5-6 (AKA Deborah's theme verses before they were cool)

# ESTHER

*"For if you remain silent at this time... who knows but that you have come to royal position for such a time as this?"*
*(Esther 4:14)*

ESTHER

# Chapter 14

# The Story of Esther

***O****R: HOW A JEWISH GIRL WON "PERSIA'S NEXT TOP WIFE" AND SAVED HER PEOPLE WITH A SIDE OF SASS*

*"For if you remain silent at this time... who knows but that you have come to royal position for such a time as this?" (Esther 4:14)*

Gather close, my friend, because this one isn't your average bedtime story. The year? 479 BC. The empire? Persia — the superpower of its day, stretching from India all the way to Africa. And on the throne sat King Xerxes, a man with more money than sense and a taste for over-the-top spectacle. This is the guy who once threw a party that lasted six whole months. Six. Months. Imagine a frat boy with unlimited funding, an open bar, and zero adult supervision. That's Xerxes.

Now, into this chaos walks Queen Vashti, his wife. And here's where things get spicy. At one of these never-ending banquets, Xerxes gets a little too tipsy and decides he wants to show her off — like a trophy wife paraded before his drunk buddies. Basically, he demands she strut her stuff in what would amount to an ancient lingerie show. And Vashti? She says no. Flat-out refuses. Cue the scandal. The king, embarrassed in front of all his friends, strips her crown and kicks her out. Say what you will, but Vashti was the original queen of boundaries.

With Vashti gone, Persia now needs a new queen. And this is where the story takes a sharp turn. Enter a young Jewish girl named Hadassah. That was her real name — Hadassah, after the myrtle tree, a symbol of peace and blessing in her people's tradition. But in a foreign land, surrounded by people who didn't worship her God, she went by another name: Esther. It was safer. More Persian-sounding. A way to blend in when standing out could cost you your life.

And here's where things get wild. Esther doesn't "apply" for the role of queen. She's drafted into it. Taken from her home, swept into the king's harem with hundreds of other girls, and forced into what can only be described as the world's most dangerous beauty pageant. Forget Miss Universe.

Forget *The Bachelor*. This was The Hunger Games dressed up with silk and jewels — and if you lost, you didn't just get sent home without a rose. You could be forgotten. Erased. Maybe even executed.

So when people talk about Esther as if she just won a glamorous pageant, don't buy it. This wasn't her dream come true. It was survival. And yet — this ordinary girl with two names, caught between two worlds, was about to step into the spotlight of history.

## FROM ORPHAN TO IT GIRL

Our story doesn't open in a palace with silken curtains and gold goblets. It begins in the Jewish quarter of Susa, tucked into the shadow of Persian grandeur, where a young girl named Hadassah lived with her cousin Mordecai. Now, Mordecai wasn't just a cousin; he was full-on "Jewish Dad™" mode.

If helicopter parenting had an ancient prototype, it was him.

Picture the scene:

Mordecai, shouting from the doorway: *"Hadassah! You are NOT leaving this house without taking a snack."*

Esther, rolling her eyes: *"I'm literally just going to the well."*

Mordecai, thrusting dried figs into her hands: *"TAKE. THE. SNACK."*

That was her life. Simple rhythms: fetch water, prep food, dodge Persian soldiers patrolling the streets, and perfect the art of not rolling her eyes when the neighborhood boys tried out their clumsy flirt lines. She was ordinary, almost invisible. Until the day her world turned upside down.

Because while Vashti's crown was gathering dust in the royal trash bin, King Xerxes was spiraling into what can only be described as a royal midlife crisis. And instead of buying a sports chariot or building a man cave, he issued a decree: *"Bring me all the beautiful virgins of the empire!"* Yep. That was Plan A. Not very original, but Xerxes was never known for subtlety.

And this wasn't an "apply if interested" kind of gig. This was armed guards pounding on doors, marching into homes, and carrying off daughters. Consent wasn't in the vocabulary. Imagine the fear in those neighborhoods: mothers clutching daughters, fathers powerless, cousins like Mordecai watching helplessly as Hadassah was taken.

The process was brutal. Step one: get kidnapped. Step two: endure twelve months of "spa treatments" — and by spa I mean a year of being scrubbed, plucked, perfumed, oiled, and polished until you glowed like a Persian lantern. Myrrh facials, oil massages, elaborate hair rituals — basically, the empire's most aggressive makeover show. Step three: spend one night with the king. Romantic? Hardly. This wasn't candlelit dinners and roses; this was state-sanctioned objectification. Step four: if he liked you, congratulations, you might be queen. If not... well, you disappeared into the endless harem, forgotten.

So when Esther's name is called, don't picture her strutting into this pageant with confidence. She wasn't a contestant; she was cargo. An orphaned girl with two names — Hadassah, her Jewish identity, tucked quietly in her heart, and Esther, the Persian name that let her blend in — swept away into the most dangerous beauty contest in history.

And yet, this nobody from Susa was about to become the "it girl" of the Persian empire.

## ESTHER'S BIG BREAK (OR BIGGEST NIGHTMARE)

Now imagine this: Esther, minding her business, when suddenly—*"Congratulations, you've been selected for Persia's Next Top Wife!"*

No audition. No callback. Just royal guards going *"You're coming with us."*

Esther: *"Uh—wait—"* Guards: *"NO BACK TALK. MOVE."*

Mordecai, watching this go down: *"Hide your Jewishness. Oh, and take a snack!"*

(Yes, even in an abduction scenario, Jewish parents *still* want you fed.)

## THE GREAT PERSIAN GLOW-UP (AKA TWELVE MONTHS OF TORTURE BEAUTY)

Now let me tell you about the most intense spa retreat in history - except instead of coming out relaxed, you came out married or disappeared from the royal records forever. Picture this:

The king's harem wasn't some sexy playground - it was a high-stakes finishing school run by terrifying eunuchs who probably whispered sweet nothings like *"That skin scrub will continue until morale improves."*

For twelve. agonizing. months. Esther endured what can only be described as ancient Persian boot camp for trophy wives:

The Myrrh Massacre Every morning began with Esther being slathered in gallons of myrrh oil until she smelled like a human incense stick. The palace aestheticians would click their tongues disapprovingly - *"More oil for this one, her elbows are practically peasant-grade."*

The Great Exfoliation Incident When the head eunuch caught Esther skipping her daily pumice stone session? Girl nearly got demoted to kitchen staff. There she was, knees scraped raw from kneeling on marble during skin treatments, thinking *"I miss the days when 'rough skin' just meant I helped Mordecai haul water."*

Palace Hunger Games The dietary rules made keto look like an all-you-can-eat buffet. One platter of figs too many and suddenly you're hearing *"The king prefers delicate flowers, not... this"* - accompanied by a sweeping hand gesture at your now-unmarriageable hips.

Meanwhile, the harem was full of girls playing mind games that would make *Real Housewives* producers blush:

- Delilah from Babylon "accidentally" spilled hot wax on Esther's favorite robe
- Persian princess Zahra spread rumors about Esther's mysterious background
- Three different girls tried bribing eunuchs for better sleeping quarters near the king's chambers

But here's what separated our girl from the sparkle-toothed competition - while others perfected their smoky eyes and practiced flattering giggles (eye roll), Esther was:

1. Memorizing the names of every provincial governor (knowledge is power)
2. Learning which wines made Xerxes chatty versus which made him sulk
3. Perfecting the art of "listening like you care" (a skill women have perfected through millennia)
4. Secretly observing who in the palace might be sympathetic to Jews

And most importantly? She never forgot Mordecai's warning whispered as the guards dragged her away: *"Hide your heritage like your life depends on it... because it does."*

The other girls thought she was just being humble about her family background. Little did they know she was playing 4D chess while they played with henna cones.

Fun historical fact: Those twelve months of beauty treatments? Scholars believe they served a dual purpose - not just enhancing appearance, but testing which girls could endure royal life without cracking under pressure. And our Esther? She aced that test while secretly fasting on Jewish holidays and whispering prayers no one else could hear.

*(Next time you complain about a bad spa day, remember Esther survived a YEAR of this nonsense - without Yelp reviews or a single friend to vent to. Now THAT'S a queen.)*

### THE BIG NIGHT

Finally... it was time.

Esther, prepped within an inch of her life, was led to the king's chambers. The stakes?

- **If he liked her?** Queen status unlocked.
- **If he didn't?** Best-case scenario: Ignored. Worst-case: *Disappeared.*

But Esther wasn't just *pretty.* **She was *strategic.***

Instead of fawning over him like others probably did, she **LET HIM TALK.**

King Xerxes, stunned that a woman actually listened to him (*shocking!*), was immediately smitten.

*"This one,"* he declared. *"I like this one."*

(Actual historians believe Esther was likely chosen because *she made him feel important*—which, let's be real, is still how most men operate today.)

## AND JUST LIKE THAT—
Former orphan. Now queen.
*"Mazel tov, Hadassah—I mean, Esther!"*

## THE PLOT THICKENS (ENTER: HAMAN, THE ORIGINAL SUPERVILLAIN)

Of course, this being the Bible, things weren't all spa days and royal banquets.

Cue Haman, the king's right-hand man and the most petty, spiteful, drama-loving villain in Persia.

His problem?

He *hated* Jews. (And honestly? Probably hated joy, puppies, and sunshine too.)

When Mordecai refused to bow to him (Jewish kingship laws said NO idolatry), Haman didn't just get mad—he went full *Disney villain*.

How far did he go?

- Schmoozed the king
- Convinced him to order a *genocide*
- Built a 75-FOOT GALLOWS in his backyard (because *of course* he did)
- Planned the mass execution for *Adar 13* (aka the luckiest *un*lucky day in Jewish history)

And Esther, sitting pretty in the palace, had NO idea her people were sentenced to die... until Mordecai sent word.

## With one message:

*"You think you're safe in that palace? Think again. This is your moment. Do something."*

Just when Esther thought she'd mastered palace life - navigating petty court politics, surviving deadly dinner parties, and perfecting her "I adore hearing about your military conquests for the seventh time, my king" face - disaster struck. And not the "someone wore my same dress to the banquet" kind.

Mordecai's message arrived via a trembling servant: "Haman has convinced the king to kill all the Jews. You're not safe either."

Esther's stomach dropped. The lavish gold bracelets on her wrists suddenly felt like shackles. That carefully constructed persona as docile Queen Esther threatened to crack open, revealing terrified Hadassah underneath.

For three sleepless nights, she paced her chambers, replaying Mordecai's warning: "Who knows but that you have come to your position for such a time as this?" The irony tasted bitter - she'd survived the harem, won the crown, only to have her people slaughtered because of one man's fragile ego?

Then came the turning point: Esther's maids found her the next morning surrounded by scrolls of Jewish prayers, her face washed of its royal cosmetics, wrapped in the plain linen of mourning.

"Prepare my attendants," she ordered quietly. "We're going to pray."

## ENTER: HISTORY'S MOST DANGEROUS SPIRITUAL PREP WORK

For three days, Esther and her closest servants:

- Fasted completely (no small feat when palace chefs kept bringing trays of almond pastries)
- Prayed in shifts rotating through all 150 Psalms (some creatively translated into Persian to avoid suspicion)
- Secretly gathered intelligence through back channels about Haman's movements
- Sewn a hidden prayer shawl into her royal gown (because sometimes you need tangible faith under all that silk)

Meanwhile outside the palace walls, Mordecai had organized the Jewish community to join this spiritual resistance - turning what looked like a death sentence into a divine showdown in the making.

We don't have Esther's exact words (the Bible leaves us hanging!), but based on Jewish tradition and the urgency of her situation, scholars believe her prayer likely included:

1. Raw honesty: "God, I'm terrified. This crown feels heavy and meaningless right now."
2. Bold petitions: "If I die, let me die standing for my people rather than hiding in silk."
3. Clever strategy: Evidence suggests she'd studied Persian law meticulously, hunting for loopholes even Haman didn't anticipate.

As dawn broke on the third day, Esther stood before her mirror. No myrrh oils this time - just the faint scent of olive oil from her anointing prayer. When she fastened the royal crown, it wasn't as a timid beauty queen, but as a woman ready to confront a king and change history.

Her final whispered words before leaving chambers? "Either way, Adonai wins. But perhaps I'll get to see it happen."

And THAT, dear reader, is how you set the stage for a prayer that brings empires to their knees. Next chapter? The royal showdown where faith meets flawless eyeliner

(Now excuse me while I practice my "brave but terrified" face in the mirror. Someone bring the cupcakes.)

# Chapter 15

# Esther's Fasting and Prayer

**O**R: HOW A JEWISH GIRL TURNED HER CLOSET INTO A WAR ROOM AND CHANGED HISTORY

"Go, gather together all the Jews who are in Susa, and fast for me. Do not eat or drink for three days, night or day. I and my attendants will fast as you do. When this is done, I will go to the king, even though it is against the law. And if I perish, I perish." Esther 4:16

### DAY 1: THE SCROLL SMUGGLERS

When Esther decided to pray, she didn't just fold her hands—she orchestrated an *underground spiritual resistance movement* right under the king's nose. Here's how it went down:

Midnight Scroll Run. Esther's most trusted maid (let's call her Sarah) had a cousin who worked in the palace kitchens. That cousin's best friend was married to a scribe in the Jewish quarter. Through this *ancient girl-code network*, Sarah smuggled in:

- A tiny scroll of Psalm 22 (*"My God, my God, why have you forsaken me?"*) sewn into her tunic
- A miniature copy of Moses' prayer from Exodus 32 (when he argued with God to save Israel)
- A clay tablet with Miriam's song (Exodus 15) etched in nearly invisible markings

*"Your Majesty,"* Sarah whispered, *"the scribe says this psalm makes kings sweat."* Esther traced the Hebrew letters with her finger: *"Perfect. We'll need that energy."*

The Trust Test Esther couldn't risk her prayer circle including palace spies. So she:

1. Had Sarah "accidentally" spill wine on three attendants
2. Watched who rushed to help vs. who ran to gossip
3. Chose only those who stayed to clean the mess

*Ancient Jewish Proverb:* Want to find loyal friends? Make a mess and see who grabs a towel.

## DAY 2: THE FASTING FIASCO

Why Three Days? In Jewish tradition:

- 3 days = The time Jonah spent in the fish (Jonah 1:17)
- 3 days = The period between death and resurrection (Hosea 6:2)
- 3 days = How long the Jews prepared before meeting God at Sinai (Exodus 19:11)

Esther was essentially saying: *"God, either revive us like Jonah, meet us like at Sinai, or we'll see You in the resurrection—but MOVE."*

The Hunger Games (Literal Edition) Palace staff kept bringing trays of:

- Honey-glazed figs
- Freshly baked bread
- Pomegranate wine

Esther's stomach growled like a lion. She countered by:

- Chewing mint leaves (an ancient appetite suppressant)
- Sipping vinegar water (a digestion disruptor)
- Having attendants fan meat smells *away* from her

When a eunuch caught her refusing food: *"The queen is...uh...cleansing for a new moon ritual!"* Sarah lied smoothly.

## DAY 3: THE PRAYER WEAPONIZED

By the third day of her fast, Esther wasn't glowing with some Instagram-ready "spiritual cleanse." She was wrecked. No food. No water. Just raw dependence on God. And that's when her prayer turned into a weapon.

### The Physical Postures

Prayer in the ancient world wasn't tidy. Esther likely threw herself flat on the marble floor, forehead pressed against the cool stone — the same posture we see hinted at in Esther 8:3, when she falls prostrate before the king. This wasn't a dainty kneel with folded hands; this was total surrender, her body saying what words could not: *"God, I have nothing left. You are my only hope."*

Her prayers probably came out more like silent screams than poetic verses. Shoulders shaking, lips moving without sound — the same way Hannah had prayed generations earlier in 1 Samuel 1:15: *"I was pouring out my soul to the Lord."* It's the kind of praying that looks awkward from the outside, but heaven leans in close.

And maybe — this is speculative, but not impossible — her hands moved as she prayed, sketching the outline of the Temple in the air. Though it had been reduced to rubble 800 miles away in Jerusalem, tracing it would have been her way of saying, *"I remember where we came from. I remember Your dwelling. Don't forget us now."*

## The Prayer Arsenal

Esther's prayers weren't made up on the spot. Jewish women knew their Scriptures. She probably drew from the great prayers of her ancestors, weaving their words into her own desperation:

- Miriam's song in Exodus 15, a victory chant after crossing the Red Sea: *"The Lord is my strength and my defense; he has become my salvation."* Deliverance when the odds were impossible.
- Hannah's prayer in 1 Samuel 2: *"He raises the poor from the dust and lifts the needy from the ash heap."* A reminder that God exalts the humble — a word Esther needed as a Jewish orphan facing down an empire.

- Moses' plea in Exodus 32: *"Turn from your fierce anger; relent and do not bring disaster on your people."* A cry for mercy when judgment seemed deserved.

Each prayer was like an arrow pulled from Israel's history and launched into her present battle.

## The Secret Sign

And then, as dawn broke on the third day, Esther may have performed an act of quiet defiance and devotion. Some Jewish traditions suggest she cut a lock of her hair, placed it in a clay jar, and whispered the covenant words: *"Remember Your covenant"* (Leviticus 26:42). To us, it might sound strange. But in her world, hair was tied to identity and dignity (cf. 1 Corinthians 11:15). Offering it up symbolized radical surrender.

It echoed the Nazirite vow of Numbers 6 — where men or women voluntarily set themselves apart to God, abstaining from wine and cutting their hair only as an offering. For Esther, surrounded by palace decadence — perfume, jewels, banquets — this was her way of saying: *"I choose to be set apart for You."*

So by the time she rose to face the king, Esther wasn't just a queen in silk. She was a woman armed with the prayers of her ancestors, a vow of surrender, and the kind of raw faith that terrifies empires.

## The Power of Packaged Prayers: When God Moves in Community

Esther didn't just pray alone — she rallied a whole nation into prayer with her. The moment Mordecai said, *"Go, gather all the Jews"* (Esther 4:16), something shifted in the spiritual atmosphere.

It wasn't just one queen crying in a palace corner anymore. It was thousands of voices rising together, every whispered prayer syncing up like heaven's own Wi-Fi. Esther weaponized worship — not as a solo act, but as a chorus.

And that principle runs all through Scripture. Look at Acts 2: when 120 believers huddled together in one room, praying in unity, the Holy Spirit descended like fire. God didn't need a crowd to show up — but He chose to pour Himself out when their hearts beat in sync. It was like heaven's Fitbit registered their unity, and suddenly, boom — tongues of fire, world changed.

Or consider Peter in Acts 12. He's chained up between guards, doors bolted, escape impossible. And what's the church doing? *"The church was earnestly praying"* (v. 5). Their prayers became an angelic jailbreak team. By the time Peter knocked on the door of the prayer meeting, they were still on their knees asking God to free him. Their prayers worked faster than their faith could catch up.

Even Jesus modeled this. Think about it — the Son of God could have prayed alone and shifted the universe. But in His darkest hour at Gethsemane, He brought Peter, James, and John with Him (Matthew 26:36–38). Why? Because shared burden means divided weight. Even Jesus wanted friends nearby when His soul was "overwhelmed with sorrow."

Now back to Esther. While she fasted with her attendants, Mordecai mobilized the people.

Picture it: merchants in the marketplace, pausing mid-haggle to whisper desperate prayers. Mothers kneading bread, lips moving with Psalms. Children, voices high and small, reciting the Shema at sundown: *"Hear, O Israel: The Lord our God, the Lord is one."* The streets of Susa became a sanctuary.

They didn't have a prayer chain — they had a prayer tsunami. And Esther stood at the center of it, not as a lone heroine, but as a spark that ignited a people.

Next crisis? Borrow Esther's playbook:

1. Group chat three faithful friends: *"Emergency prayer summit—my place, 7pm. Bring soup."*
2. Assign Scripture *"war posts"* (Exodus 14:14 for one, Psalm 91 for another)
3. Agree in prayer like Jesus taught (Matthew 18:19-20)

Holy momentum happens when God's people sync hearts before His throne.

## WHY THIS PRAYER STRATEGY ABSOLUTELY DEMOLISHED THE OPPOSITION

So let me tell you why Esther's prayer approach didn't just work—it completely obliterated every spiritual barrier standing in her way. Girl didn't just knock on heaven's door; she practically kicked it down with her royal sandals.

It Cost Her Everything. Think about it—seventy-two hours without a single grape, pomegranate, or even a sip of honeyed wine while living in a palace where refusing the king's feast could literally get you executed. She was essentially betting her crown, her life, and her entire future on God showing up. Plus, by Jewish law, all that fasting made her ceremonially unclean right when she needed to look most presentable. Talk about going all-in when the stakes couldn't be higher.

It Created a Spiritual Army Every single Jewish person in Susa joined her fast. We're talking about an entire community synchronized in prayer—merchants closing their shops to pray, mothers teaching their children to fast, elderly rabbis and young workers all united in desperate intercession. When that many people align their hearts toward heaven simultaneously, you don't just get answered prayer—you get spiritual earthquakes that shake empires.

It Combined Strategy with Spirituality While she was on her knees praying, her mind was also working overtime planning that legendary dinner party trap for Haman. She literally prepared her "if I perish, I perish" speech between worship sessions, making sure every word would hit maximum impact. This wasn't passive waiting—this was active faith that trusted God while also doing the practical groundwork for breakthrough.

Let me set the scene: It's high noon in Susa. Esther's three-day prayer vigil just ended. Her knees ache from marble floors, her stomach's growling like a caged lion, and her makeup is still blotchy from holy Ugly Crying™. She smooths her royal robes with trembling hands when—

**BAM.**

## THE SCEPTER EXTENSION (Esther 5:2)

As Esther steps into the throne room (illegally!), she's halfway through rehearsing her "If I die, I die" speech when Xerxes—the man who executed his last wife for disobedience—does something shocking.

His scepter whooshes down so fast, the royal jewelers probably got whiplash. And here's the kicker:

Ancient Court Protocol Nugget: Persian law demanded queens wait months for royal summons. Yet God rewrote protocol mid-stride, proving "The king's heart is a stream of water in the Lord's hand" (Proverbs 21:1).

Xerxes, suddenly extra chatty: "Esther, baby! You look... uh... spiritually radiant?" (He's confused by her lack of eyeliner but weirdly into it.)

## HAMAN'S HOMEMADE GALLOWS (Esther 5:9-14; 7:10)

Now, while Esther was quietly fasting and plotting her bold move, Haman was stewing like a pot left too long on the fire. Ever since Mordecai refused to bow, this man had been marinating in rage. It wasn't enough for him to hate one man; he wanted an entire people wiped off the map. That's what bitterness does — it snowballs until it takes over your whole imagination.

So picture this: Esther invites the king and Haman to a dinner party — a stroke of genius on her part. Meanwhile, Haman walks in puffed up like a peacock, convinced he's the VIP of the empire. Between sips of wine, he starts bragging about his wealth, his promotions, his access to the king, and oh, by the way, that whole little side hustle of genocide he had cooking. Pride, party of one.

But that wasn't enough for him. Back home, he decides Mordecai can't wait. He orders a gallows built — not your average wooden structure, but a 75-foot monster that would've towered over the city skyline. Imagine the neighbors: *"Hey, Haman, are you putting up a watchtower?"* Nope. Just casually constructing a death machine for one stubborn Jew. Persian Home Depot must've been suspicious with all that lumber going missing.

Fast forward to Esther's second banquet. The wine is flowing, the king is mellow, and Esther finally drops the bomb: *"Spare my life... and the life of my people"* (Esther 7:3–4). The room goes silent. Xerxes, furious, storms out to cool down. Haman, realizing his goose is cooked, panics and throws himself onto Esther's couch to beg for mercy. Worst. Timing. Ever. Because that's the exact moment the king storms back in. And what does he see? His right-hand man sprawled across the queen.

Cue Xerxes bellowing: *"MY BROTHER IN ZOROASTER, ARE YOU ASSAULTING THE QUEEN TOO?!"* (Okay, maybe not verbatim, but you get the vibe).

And here's where divine comedy kicks in. The guards drag Haman out, and someone pipes up: *"By the way, there's a gallows he built for Mordecai."* The king doesn't hesitate. *"Hang him on it."* And just like that, the empire's most feared man becomes the punchline of his own twisted construction project. Executed on his own DIY gallows — hanged by his pride, paranoia, and proximity.

God's justice has a sense of irony. The trap Haman set became his undoing.

## THE LEGAL LOOPHOLE THAT LYNCHED A CURSE (Esther 8:8-14)

Here's the tricky part of Esther's story that often gets skipped in Sunday School: Persian law was airtight.

Once a decree went out under the king's seal, it was basically immortalized in stone. Not even Xerxes himself could revoke it (see Daniel 6:8 for the same problem with Daniel and the lions' den). Haman's genocide order was still on the books — a legal death sentence with a countdown timer.

So what had Esther really been fasting and praying over those three long days? Not just "God, please make Xerxes nice." She needed divine strategy. She knew Persian law couldn't be undone... but maybe it could be outmaneuvered.

And here's where it gets brilliant. Esther remembers the fine print: the king could authorize a counter-decree. In other words, she couldn't erase Haman's order, but she could overwrite it. Like when you can't delete a cursed email, but you can hit "reply all" with a better attachment.

So she makes her pitch: let the Jews defend themselves. The wording of the new edict was clear — *"the king's edict granted the Jews in every city the right to assemble and protect themselves"* (Esther 8:11). Translation: "Come at us if you want, but we're legally allowed to throw hands first."

And Xerxes? He doesn't just agree. He doubles down. Prideful as always, he essentially says, "Yeah, those are *my* Jews. They fight for me now.

Fight them, you fight me." He sends out the new decree by royal courier, galloping across the empire on the fastest horses in the stable — the ancient Persian version of hitting "send to all" with high priority.

The real miracle wasn't just legal cleverness. It was that God used the pride of a pagan king to protect His people. Xerxes got to look like a savior, but behind the scenes, it was God writing the edits. What looked like a loophole was really a lifeline.

So the curse that was meant to destroy the Jews? It got lynched by its own legal system. The empire's paperwork bowed to heaven's providence.

## WHY THIS STILL SLAPS TODAY

Esther's story isn't just an ancient Persian drama — it's a blueprint for us. God still moves when His people fast and pray, not just quietly but strategically, boldly, and *together*. When heaven hears a chorus instead of a whisper, things shift fast.

And here's the reminder: the enemy's pride always becomes his downfall. Scripture puts it this way: *"Whoever digs a pit will fall into it; if someone rolls a stone, it will roll back on them"* (Proverbs 26:27). Haman built gallows for Mordecai and ended up dangling on his own DIY project. That's not just irony; that's God's justice.

Even the strongest laws and systems bow to God's higher court. Isaiah 54:17 reminds us: *"No weapon formed against you shall prosper, and you will refute every tongue that accuses you."* Haman's decree was ironclad, but heaven out-lawyered it. And the same God who flipped an empire's paperwork for Esther still flips tables, policies, and circumstances for His people today.

So here's why Esther's story still slaps: it reminds us that prayer is not a last resort — it's the opening move. That arrogance will always tie its own noose. And that no earthly system, no matter how permanent it seems, gets the final word. God does.

*(Now if you'll excuse me, I'm off to dramatically whisper psalms into my houseplants. They're my captive audience.)*

# Chapter 16

# Lessons from Esther's Prayer

**OR: SURVIVAL TACTICS FOR WHEN YOU'RE OUTNUMBERED BUT NOT OUTPRAYED**

*"For the vision is yet for an appointed time... though it tarries, wait for it." (Habakkuk 2:3, Esther's version: 'Plot twists take reservations')*

Grab Your Popcorn, This Gets Good. Alright sisters, gather 'round the holy campfire while I tell you why Esther's prayer strategy is like the ultimate Marvel movie plot - except with less spandex and more divine intervention.

Picture this: Our girl Esther wasn't just sitting in her royal chambers gently folding her hands like some porcelain princess. Oh no, honey. She was running spiritual special ops from a palace that made the White House look like a Motel 6.

Her prayer life made Navy Seals look like boy scouts - and here's why:

That Hebrew word for fasting? "Sum"? Not only did it mean going without food, it literally translated to "to put to silence." So when Esther called that fast, she wasn't just asking for help - she was muzzle-loading heaven's artillery against her enemies.

Kinda like when you try to fast from social media to focus on God but keep "accidentally" checking Instagram - except Esther actually followed through. No cheating with Persian snack cakes hidden under the royal duvet for this queen!

### Her three-pronged attack:

1. **Divine Intel** - She didn't just pray blindfolded. She studied Persian law like it was the syllabus for Survival 101 (which it kinda was).
2. **Girl Squad** - Her maids weren't just doing her hair - they were intercessors in disguise, probably whispering Psalms while brushing out her extensions.
3. **Backup Plan** - She went into that throne room with a "if this goes south" play that would make Jason Bourne proud.

Now here's the kicker - she turned a beauty queen pageant survival strategy into a nation-saving military campaign. Male generals would've charged in swords swinging. Esther? She prayed first, THEN let her lipstick be her weapon.

The lesson? Effective prayer isn't about looking holy - it's about getting strategic.

Ever had that friend who plans girls trips like they're invading Normandy? The one with color-coded spreadsheets and backup ponchos just in case? That's Esther - but for spiritual warfare.

Next time you're facing impossible odds, remember: Your prayer closet isn't for whimpering - **it's your war room.** And honey, there's no crown too heavy for a woman who knows how to mix faith with holy strategy.

Fun Bible Easter Egg: That "sum" fasting - same word used when God silenced Egypt's armies at the Red Sea. Coincidence? Or is God low-key telling us fasting is His secret weapon against bullies?

## SPIRITUAL TRUTHS (WITH EXTRA SASS)

Prayer is Lotion for Destiny Spots Esther's three-day glow-up wasn't about beauty - it was spiritual prep. While her face was breaking out from fasting, her *faith* was clearing up (Esther 4:16).

Divine Delays ≠ Divine Denials For TWELVE MONTHS Esther prepped in that harem before her "suddenly" moment (Esther 2:12). God was marinating her for the main course.

The Best Prayers Have Footnotes Esther's *"if I perish"* prayer included legal research on Persian statutes (Esther 8:8). Girl came with receipts!
*Imagine: "Lord, free my people... also here's subsection 4B of the legal code we can use, amen."*

## PRAYER PRACTICE: SWIPE ESTHER'S MOVES

The "Esther Envelope" Challenge:

Find an old perfume bottle (Esther 2:12 vibes). Each morning:

- Write one fear on paper ("Haman's plot") - One thing you wish to defeat or over come.
- Drip a dab of perfume on it (representing prayer) - but actually pray over it. You can't spray the perfume if you never prayed. - Continue to pray over it and each time spray some perfume
- Seal it with "For Such a Time as this" (Esther 4:14)
- Remove the fear when the time comes to remember how many things God has helped you over come. Maybe you can stamp it with lipstick to proclaim how God helped you over come.
- **Its nice to see how amazing God has been in our life, we get so busy, we easily forget what God has overcome for us.**

Watch how God makes your fears smell nice.

Esther's Prayer Posse (and Yours Too)

Let's get real: Esther did not waltz into that throne room as a one-woman army. No ma'am. She had her ride-or-dies, her prayer posse, her holy huddle. These weren't just ladies-in-waiting fluffing pillows and brushing her hair — they were her spiritual emergency contacts, the ones who held the ropes when she went over the cliff (Exodus 17:12 vibes). Esther knew this truth in her bones: you don't storm enemy territory without backup.

Picture her inner circle for a moment. The Prayer Warrior — probably the oldest maid, eyes sharp, making sure no one cheated on the fast. The Intel Gatherer — tuned in to palace gossip, not for drama but for strategy, tucking away every overheard detail like holy espionage. And the Muscle — the girl who could carry a basin of water with one hand and, let's be honest, probably had a dagger tucked into her sash. These women didn't just serve Esther; they stood with her. When she fasted, they fasted.

When she trembled, they interceded. When she stepped into that throne room knowing death was a real possibility, they were back in her chambers still praying, still holding the line, still lifting her up to God.

And here's where it hits home: some of us don't have a circle like that. Maybe friendships fell away. Maybe life got busy. Maybe you've been the strong one for so long, you forgot you're allowed to need others. But here's the promise: God is faithful to provide. Pray for Him to send the right people — women who chase Him, who will chase after you when you drift, who will stand watch over your purpose like it's their own. Don't underestimate His ability to knit hearts together. The book of Ecclesiastes says it straight: *"Two are better than one... if either of them falls down, one can help the other up"* (Ecclesiastes 4:9–10).

So, what does this look like for you? Build your own prayer task force. Find your 3 A.M. Crew — the friend who answers the phone at midnight and shows up in pajamas with prayer on her lips. Find your Encourager — the one who refuses to let you spiral, sending you Scripture when you're ready to microwave your problems (and your dignity). Find your Doer — the one who shows up with a casserole, cash, or a crowbar, depending on what the crisis calls for. These are not casual contacts. These are lifelines.

When do you call them in? When your boss is acting like Haman and you feel cornered. When your marriage, your health, or your peace is under attack (John 10:10 reminds us the enemy comes to "steal, kill, and destroy"). When God is stirring something so new in you that you need someone to confirm, *"Yes girl, that really was the Holy Spirit — not the tacos."*

And here's the kicker: Esther's maids fasted and prayed with no guarantee they'd even live to see the outcome. They prayed blind, trusting that if she won, they all won. That's real sisterhood. That's kingdom friendship.

So don't wait for crisis mode. Pray for your people now. Nurture those relationships now. And when the day comes that you have to stand before your own "king," text your crew: *"Emergency prayer summit. My place. Bring coffee, your Bible, and maybe a spiritual flamethrower. We've got work to do."*

Because here's the secret Esther teaches us: victory rarely comes to the lone warrior. It comes to the praying community that dares to believe together.

## BLESSING (OR WHY YOU'RE ALREADY WINNING)

Sweet sister, lean in close — because if God could use a kidnapped orphan in a corrupt, sexist system stacked against her, He can absolutely work through you too. Esther wasn't perfect. She was scared. She hesitated. She lived with a secret identity. And yet God wove every messy thread of her story into something unstoppable.

So yes, He can use your tear-stained prayers, your questionable choices, even that moment you broke your fast a little too early because bread was calling your name. None of it disqualifies you. In fact, it makes you the perfect candidate for His grace to shine.

Esther's story ends with a loophole no one saw coming. That's God's specialty. When His people pray boldly and strategically, He doesn't just play by the world's rules — He rewrites them mid-game. What was meant to crush you? He flips it into your victory. What was signed and sealed against you? He edits with His own hand.

So here's your blessing: You are already more victorious than you know. You don't have to have it all together. You just have to be willing to show up, like Esther did, trembling but trusting. And heaven will do the rest.

*(Now go forth and make your next prayer meeting look like a NATO summit. Spiritual warfare loves a good spreadsheet.)*

# HAGAR

*"You are the God who sees me"*
*(Genesis 16:13)*

# Chapter 17

# The Story of Hagar

***O****R: THAT TIME A SLAVE GIRL OUT-THEOLOGIZED THE PATRIARCHS AND LIVED TO TELL THE TALE*

*"You are the God who sees me" (Genesis 16:13, first recorded instance of a woman naming God in Scripture - mic drop!)*

**THE DESERT WASN'T ON HER VISION BOARD**

The sand burned between Hagar's toes as she adjusted the heavy water jug against her hip. This wasn't her dream. Truthfully, Hagar had stopped dreaming a long time ago. She'd been born into bondage — or maybe captured during one of those endless Egyptian border wars with Canaan. No one asked her opinion on the matter. Her life wasn't chosen; it was handed to her like a chain.

In Pharaoh's palace she was just another face among the slave girls, grinding grain until her arms ached, scrubbing marble floors until her skin cracked, doing what she could to survive in a world that never once asked her what she wanted. Egypt was all she knew: the smell of the Nile mud, the bustle of Memphis streets, the chants to gods who never answered.

And then — everything shifted. Some Hebrew wanderer named Abram showed up with his too-beautiful wife Sarai, and Pharaoh (after making one *very awkward mistake* about who was married to whom) decided to smooth things over with parting gifts. Livestock, silver, gold... and Hagar. One day she belonged to Pharaoh; the next she was shoved into a caravan as part of the "sorry we kidnapped your wife" peace basket.

From then on, her life was tethered to tents. No more palace kitchens. No city streets. Just a nomadic camp in Canaan, where she fetched water before dawn and listened to Sarai mutter about how the humidity ruined her hairpieces. Every day was service: jars of water hauled until her back screamed, ceremonial robes washed and rewashed until her fingers wrinkled, meals prepared under the hot breath of desert winds.

"A dozen more jars before noon," the steward barked. "And Lady Sarai says the traveling robes still smell like camel. Do them again."

Across camp, Abram busied himself with his flocks, careful never to meet her eyes. Again.

**Modern equivalent?** Imagine getting transferred from your barista job at Starbucks to Elon Musk's Mars colony... only to become his wife's personal maid and (spoiler alert) her substitute womb.

## THE BACHELORETTE: ANCIENT NEAR EAST EDITION

One morning, Sarai's tent flap snapped open like a whip. *"Hagar. We need to talk."*

The "talk" was less conversation, more command. Sarai was tired of waiting on God's promise. Abram needed an heir. Hagar had a functioning uterus. Simple math.

"What could go wrong?" Sarai mused, drizzling goat's milk over her barley cakes as if she wasn't about to upend three lives and ignite centuries of family drama.

Hagar swallowed hard. As a slave, refusal wasn't an option. Consent wasn't in her contract.

That night, Abram came to her tent, avoiding her eyes as he rolled onto her sleeping mat. She lay still, staring at the ceiling, the desert wind rattling the tent poles, wondering how a girl from Memphis had ended up here: a body pressed into service, a pawn in someone else's story.

### When Pregnancy Glow Meets Toxic Workplace

Three moons later, Hagar's body betrayed her secret. Her belly rounded gently, her skin flushed with that unmistakable glow. At first, it was just whispers among the other servants as she passed the well.

*"Think she'll get her own tent now?"*
*"Please. Pharaoh's daughter got ten new handmaids last week. Hagar'll be lucky if she gets a new pillow."*

The gossip swirled like desert dust, rising and stinging, impossible to avoid.

But the real storm came from Sarai. What started as cold stares turned into impossible demands. Every request dripped with venom, like poison disguised as honey.

*"This woven mat is far too rough for my delicate son."*
*"Why does my foot bath taste like sand?"*
*"Are you smirking at me, girl?"*

Hagar bit her tongue. Day after day, she carried water, scrubbed garments, and kneaded bread with swollen ankles and an aching back, all while enduring Sarai's sharpened words. But the final straw came one afternoon when Abram—yes, the "father of many nations"—fumbled spectacularly at sheep shearing. Hagar let slip the tiniest laugh. Sarai's hand struck her cheek so fast the stars burst in her vision.

This wasn't just a spat between two women. It was war inside a toxic household. And Hagar, the slave girl from Egypt, was caught in the crossfire of someone else's desperation for a child.

## Cultural context matters here.

Archaeologists have uncovered clay tablets from Nuzi, an ancient Mesopotamian city, detailing surrogate contracts. They spell it out: if a wife couldn't bear children, she could give her maid to her husband, and the child born would legally belong to the wife. Sounds familiar, right? But here's the kicker—none of those contracts ever address what happens if the surrogate herself becomes a threat. None talk about jealousy boiling over.

None imagine the barren wife might mistreat the very woman carrying her hope. And certainly none prepare us for what Hagar endured next: a pregnant woman, driven into the desert, her life and her baby's hanging by a thread.

Hagar may have been "just a servant" in her master's eyes, but her story shows us the cracks in the system. She wasn't a contract. She was a woman, pregnant, hurting, and seen by the God who writes stories no culture can erase.

## Runner Runner (But Make It Theological)

Barefoot and bleeding, Hagar bolted into the wilderness until the campfires behind her blurred into nothing but memory. Each step pounded out a rhythm: *don't look back, don't look back.* The desert night swallowed her whole, silence pressing in except for her ragged breaths.

By the time she reached the edge of Shur, she collapsed beside what generously counted as an "oasis": three sad palm trees and a puddle so questionable even the camels were like, *"Hard pass."*

She rubbed her swollen belly and muttered, *"Maybe the jackals will be kinder."*

And then—stage left—God entered.

Only, He didn't storm in with trumpets or lightning. He sent an angel who called her by name: *"Hagar, slave-girl of Sarai..."*

Cue eye-roll. Inside, Hagar bristled. *"Oh great, another man with demands. Haven't I had enough of those?"*

But instead of orders, came promises. God said, *"I will multiply your offspring until they outnumber Walmart shoppers on Black Friday."* (Okay, maybe not in those exact words, but close: Genesis 16:10.)

**Theological Mic Drop:** This is the very first time in Scripture that God personally promises blessing to a Gentile woman. Not Abram. Not Sarai. Hagar. An Egyptian slave girl running for her life. That's not just comfort — that's rebellion against the patriarchal playbook of the ancient world.

### THE ULTIMATE VINDICATION

Dust clung to Hagar's tear-streaked cheeks, her sleeve crusted with snot. She sat under that stubborn desert sun, the same sun that had witnessed every humiliation of her life — Pharaoh's slave quarters, Sarai's jealous tirades, Abram's silence. And for the first time, she whispered something bold:

*"Fine. But I'm naming You."*

She didn't have Abram's theology degree. She didn't have Sarai's pedigree. But she had what neither of them dared — the audacity to give God a name. And her cracked lips shaped it:

*"El Roi. The God Who Sees Me."*

The absurdity nearly made her laugh. Years of being invisible — just another servant, another womb, another body to be used — and the first Being to truly notice her was the Creator of the universe. Not because she was carrying Abram's heir. Not because she was strategically important. But simply because she existed.

And then came the kicker: *"Go back."*

## Record scratch.

Go back? To Sarai, who slapped her? To Abram, who wouldn't even look her in the eye? To the tents where she'd forever be "that Egyptian," a body on loan? Every muscle in her body screamed *no*.

But beneath the fury, something new stirred. Because this wasn't just a command — it was a commission. She wasn't going back as disposable property. She was going back seen, chosen, carrying promises bigger than the desert sky.

Hagar trudged home with fire in her bones. Yes, she'd still haul water, still chop wood, still dodge Sarai's glares. But now, every time she whispered a prayer, she knew her name was written in heaven's margins. Not as footnote. As headline.

While the patriarchs were still fumbling their way through doubt and negotiation, Hagar — a foreign, enslaved, pregnant runaway — was out here rewriting theology:

She's the first person in Scripture to name God (Genesis 16:13).
She receives unconditional promises (Genesis 21:18) — no strings attached, no contracts signed.
She experiences a resurrection metaphor centuries before Jesus, when God opens her eyes to a well of water just as her son is dying (Genesis 21:19).

And she did all this while society called her expendable.

\*\*\*

## MIRACLE BABIES AND SIDE-EYES AT THE BUFFET TABLE

Seventeen years is a long time in the desert. Within those years, a whole soap opera unfolded. First came the shocker: Sarah — the woman who literally laughed in God's face at the idea of nursing a baby — actually got pregnant (Genesis 18:12, Genesis 21:2). Cue the world's most awkward gender reveal: no confetti cannons, just Abraham announcing, "It's a boy!" while Sarah tried not to choke on her goat milk.

Then, as if that weren't enough drama, God told Abraham that every male in the household needed to be circumcised (Genesis 17:10–11). Imagine calling a staff meeting for that announcement. Ishmael was thirteen at the time, probably planning to sleep in, when suddenly his dad shows up with a flint knife and a very nervous look. Somewhere in the tents, teenage boys muttered, *"This covenant thing is getting way too personal."*

Fast forward four years later: Abraham's hundredth birthday bash doubles as Isaac's weaning party. The whole camp is decked out desert chic — colorful woven drapes billowing, lamb chops sizzling over open fire pits, honey cakes stacked high. Abraham beams like a man who finally got the child he's been bragging about for decades. He puffs out his chest, parades Isaac around, and introduces him to every guest like a miracle on two chubby legs.

Meanwhile, in the corner...

Ishmael, seventeen, hormonal, and over it, watches the fuss with narrowed eyes. *"Wow. Dad suddenly remembers how to throw parties now that his 'real son' shows up."* He flicks a grape toward Isaac's cradle with just enough spite to make it sting.

Hagar, sitting beside him, elbows him hard. *"Shhh! We're on thin mat rations as it is."*

But Sarah's hawk-eyes miss nothing. Across the tent, her gaze zeroes in like a predator spotting prey. Cue: The Most Dramatic Eye Roll in Genesis (Genesis 21:9). Modern translation? Replace the grapes with TikTok drama and you've got every blended-family Thanksgiving dinner, ancient edition.

## THE KICK-HEARD-'ROUND-CANAAN

Sarah had had it. She stormed into Abraham's tent like a woman whose patience had just expired. *"Get this slave woman and her son out of here! He's not splitting the inheritance with my miracle baby."* (Genesis 21:10 — Housewives of Canaan, Episode 2.)

Abraham froze. He loved Ishmael. The boy was his firstborn, his blood. But Sarah had waited ninety years for her child — and now she wasn't about to share. The air in the tent grew heavy. Abraham shuffled. Ishmael fumed. Hagar stayed silent.

Then God broke the silence: *"Do what Sarah says. I'll take care of them."* (Genesis 21:12–13).

And here's the kicker — Sarah wasn't just being petty (though, let's be real, the jealousy was thicker than camel stew). In the ancient world, the firstborn son held legal rights to a double portion of inheritance. Ancient Mesopotamian tablets spell it out: the eldest son got the lion's share, even if the second wife produced another heir. Sarah knew the law, and she played it ruthless.

So yes, her words were sharp. But under the drama, a deeper battle was being waged: God's promise wasn't going to be split down the middle. Isaac would carry the covenant line — and Ishmael, though sent away, would still become a great nation of his own. Two stories, diverging, but both still under heaven's eye.

## THE BOOT LIST

Hagar's eviction notice included:
One waterskin (half-full)
Stale bread (possibly repurposed from the party platter)
Abraham's "blessing" (*"Try not to die!"*)
Zero camels
Ishmael (as they trudged into the desert): *"So... God's still got that 'make you a great nation' promise, right?"*

## When a Mother's Gutsy Sob Session Changed History)

The desert sun beat down like a merciless creditor, demanding payment in sweat and sanity. Hagar's cracked lips stung as she poured the last few drops from the limp waterskin onto Ishmael's parched tongue. The boy—her boy, almost a man but suddenly so small—moaned weakly.

Two truths clenched her heart like a fist:

1. They weren't going to make it.
2. Ishmael didn't know that yet.

*"Rest here,"* she whispered, dragging him toward a scraggly broom tree (basically tumbleweed with a superiority complex). Its shade was more placebo than protection, but at least it gave the illusion of shelter.

Not pictured in Sunday school books:

The moment she realized Ishmael was too dehydrated to even cry.
The way her arms still ached with phantom memory of nursing him, though her milk had long dried up.
The tactical genius of her "walking away" (Genesis 21:15).

This wasn't surrender. It was the last defiant act of a mother who refused to let her son watch her faith shatter.

When she'd stumbled far enough that he couldn't hear her sobs, Hagar crumpled behind a dune. And what came out wasn't polished prayer—it was desperate bargaining.

*"Take me instead."* (But God already had a plan.)
*"I'll walk back to Egypt."* (Three hundred miles of sand without water? Impossible.)
Finally: *"Just don't make me watch."*

Then came the seven words that split the heavens wide open:

**"I can't watch him die. I just can't."**

That was it. No titles. No poetry. No careful theology. Just the guttural cry of a mother whose vocabulary had run out. And that's why it wrecked the heavenly boardroom.

No Titles. She didn't butter God up with "O Sovereign Lord, Creator of Heaven and Earth." She screamed to the same God who had once seen her under a different desert sky (Genesis 16:13).

No Theology. No reminders about covenants or promises. Just raw maternal terror.

No Posture. She wasn't kneeling reverently. She was curled fetal-style in the dirt, body shaking, face streaked with salt and dust.

It was the desert equivalent of that midnight ER sob when your kid's fever won't break and you're too exhausted to form coherent sentences. Heaven doesn't require eloquence—it recognizes rupture.

And here's the kicker: God answered before she even finished. While she wept, an angel was already nudging open an underground aquifer (Genesis 21:19). Not because Hagar prayed "right." Not because she deserved it. But because she was seen.

## GOD'S RESPONSE (AND FIRST RECORDED WATER HACK)

The angel's words were simple: *"Get up, Mama. Lift the boy. I've got a well over here."* (Genesis 21:18–19).

Hagar blinked, confused. *"Wait—that crack in the ground was here the whole time?"*

Fun desert fact: geologists today confirm that limestone fissures in Beersheba trap underground water. God didn't create a spring out of thin air. He opened Hagar's eyes to what despair had blinded her to. Provision was already there. She just couldn't see it through her tears.

Ishmael lived. Not just survived—thrived. He grew up in the wilderness, mastered the bow (Genesis 21:20), and became the father of twelve princes (Genesis 25:12–16).
Abraham's "extra" son turned into the patriarch of nations.

Because in God's economy, the rejected don't stay rejected. They become the living proof that His promises outlast our mess.

Sweet sister, if God could find Hagar weeping in the dirt — hungry, homeless, and convinced she was finished — then He sees you too. He doesn't wait for you to pull yourself together or find the perfect words.

He shows up in the middle of your ugly-cry, when your mascara's streaked and your sentences don't make sense. That's when heaven leans in.

Hagar thought she was disposable. God called her indispensable. She thought she was forgotten. God wrote her into history.

She thought she was unseen. God gave her His name: *El Roi — the God Who Sees Me.*

So here's your blessing: may you know deep in your bones that you are never invisible to Him. May your cracked whispers rise like thunder in heaven's courts. May the wells of provision hidden in your wilderness spring open before your eyes. And may you walk back into your life — not as the cast-off, not as the overlooked — but as the one God Himself stopped for.

Because if He saw Hagar, He sees you too.

*(Now if you'll excuse me, I need to chug three waterskins in solidarity. Motherhood is* **hard.***)*

# Chapter 18

# Hagar's Wilderness Whispers

**O**R: WHEN "PLEASE DON'T LET MY BABY DIE" BECAME HISTORY'S SHORTEST POWERFUL PRAYER

*"She went off and sat down about a bowshot away, for she thought, 'Let me not see the child die.' And she sat opposite him and lifted up her voice and wept." (Genesis 21:16)*

## THE BREAKING POINT: WHEN THE DESERT TRIED TO CLAIM THEM

Gather close, friends, and let me tell you about the day the sun itself seemed to lean down and press its fiery thumb against a mother and her child.

Three days.

Three endless days of stumbling through the furnace of Beersheba, where the very air tasted like baked dust and regret. Hagar's sandals had long since fallen apart—not that it mattered when the ground burned hotter than Pharaoh's furnaces. The waterskin at her side hung limp, lighter than a whisper, its last few precious drops given to Ishmael hours ago.

And oh, Ishmael.

Her boy—once so full of fire, so quick with a laugh—now lay beneath a scraggly broom bush, his breath coming in shallow gasps. His lips, once quick to tease, were cracked like sunbaked pottery. His skin, once warm with youth, now stretched too tight over his bones.

And the vultures?

They circled.

Not yet diving, not yet bold—but watching. Waiting. Making silent bets on how much longer this woman and her son could last.

Hagar knew the math.

No water. No shade. No mercy.

This was the desert's way—slow, cruel, indifferent.
And yet.
And yet.

When she looked at her son—her boy—something inside her, something deeper than fear, deeper than despair, deeper than the ache in her legs and the burn in her throat, snapped.

She couldn't watch this.
She wouldn't.
So she did the only thing left to do.

She dragged Ishmael into the meager shade of that broom bush—"Stay here, my love"—and then she walked away.

Not to abandon him.
Never that.
But because no mother wants her child to see her break.
And oh, she was breaking.
She stumbled just far enough that he wouldn't hear her scream.

And then—

Then, with the vultures wheeling overhead and the sand biting her knees, Hagar, the slave girl, the cast-off, the woman the world had tried to erase, lifted her face to the heavens...

...and howled.

Not a prayer.
Not a plea.

A raw, unfiltered, unbearable cry from the depths of a mother's shattered soul:

**"I CAN'T WATCH HIM DIE."**

Seven words.
That's all it was.

Seven words, torn from her throat like a piece of her own flesh.

No fancy titles for God. No polished theology. No bargaining.

Just the truth, ugly and desperate and alive.

And heaven—
Heaven stopped.

Because sometimes, the most powerful prayers aren't the pretty ones.

Sometimes, they're the ones that sound like a woman screaming into the void, demanding to be heard.
And Hagar?

Oh, Hagar was done being silent.

What finally snapped her? Probably:

Ishmael's whimpers turning to whimpers ("I'm just...so...thirsty...")
Realizing Abraham's God might be like every other man who'd failed them
That soul-crushing moment when you realize this might be it

## THE PRAYER THAT CRACKED THE SKY OPEN

Let me tell you something about prayers—real prayers, the kind that don't come from Sunday school books but from the raw, unfiltered guts of a human soul. Hagar's prayer wasn't poetry. It wasn't liturgy. It wasn't even a sentence, really—not the kind you'd write down neatly in a journal.

No.
This was a howl.
Seven Hebrew words. Seven syllables torn from a woman's throat like flesh from bone.

**"Al tiri b'mot hana'ar."**
(Let me not see the child's death.)

Now, if we're being honest, most translations clean it up, make it sound more reverent than it was. But let's break this down like archaeologists sifting through the wreckage of a broken heart.

### THE WORDS THEMSELVES: A LINGUISTIC EARTHQUAKE

**"Al tiri"** (אַל־תִּרְאִי)

The "Al" is a raw prohibition—not just "don't," but "Don't you dare." The kind of word you spit through clenched teeth when you're cornered.

"Tiri" comes from the verb "to see"—but not casual observation. This is witnessing horror. The same phrase shows up when Lot begs the angels not to make him flee to the mountains (Genesis 19:19). It's the cry of someone who cannot bear to look.

**Modern equivalent?** Imagine whispering to a friend in the ER waiting room: "Don't make me watch him die."

### "B'mot" (בְּמוֹת)

The "b'" prefix turns "mot" (death) into something even more visceral—it's death in the act of happening. Not "dying," but actively being murdered by circumstance.

The root "mut" appears in Job's most desperate laments—the kind of death that smothers, that doesn't come gently.

**Modern equivalent?** That gasp you suck in when your kid coughs up blood. When the bad news hits like a punch to the ribs.

### "Ha'na'ar" (הַנַּעַר)

"The boy." Not "my son." Not "Ishmael." Just... the boy.

In Hebrew, dropping possessives is devastating. It means the speaker can't even claim ownership anymore. it's too painful. He's just a child now. Generic. Expendable.

**Modern equivalent?** The way ER nurses refer to "the patient" instead of "your husband." Distance for survival.

## What She Didn't Say

No "O Lord."
No "If it be Thy will."
Not even "God."

She doesn't address the Almighty. She howls into the silence—not because she doubts He's there, but because she doesn't have breath left for titles.

The Hebrew says "she lifted her voice and wept" (וַתִּשָּׂא אֶת־קֹלָהּ וַתֵּבְךְּ).

But "lifted" (nasa) here isn't choir practice. It's the same verb used for heaving stones onto a burial cairn. And "wept" (bakah)? Not delicate sniffles. This is snot-choked, full-body disintegration.

Picture it:

- A woman facedown in the dirt.
- Fingers clutching at sand like it might become water.
- A scream so guttural it barely forms words.

**This isn't prayer. This is labor.**

The kind that births miracles.

### Why It Worked

Because God doesn't need eloquence.
He needs honesty.
And Hagar?
Oh, she was honest.

### GOD'S UNEXPECTED MOVE

Angel's Surprising Approach: Doesn't lead with comfort - just facts:

1. "What troubles you, Hagar?" (Gen 21:17) - Like saying "State your case" to a lawyer

2. Repeats the exact promise from 16:11 ("I will make him a nation")
3. Then shows the well that was there all along (Gen 21:19)

God doesn't apologize for the suffering - just proves He never left.

Let me tell you what happens after the miracle—because miracles aren't the end. They're the beginning.

The Bible doesn't give us a timeline, but any desert-dweller knows: you don't gulp water after days without it. You sip. You let your body remember what life tastes like.

So picture it:

- **Hour 1:** Hagar probably brings him some water then when he is strong enough, he probably stumbles to the well. Ishmael's cracked lips press to the water's edge. His hands shake so badly Hagar has to cup them for him.
- **Day 1:** The boy sleeps—really sleeps—for the first time since they were cast out. His breath steadies. His color returns.
- **Then** They fill the waterskin to the brim. The vultures have flown off.

And then?

They walk.

Not back to Abraham. Not to grovel. But forward, into the wilderness of Paran—a place so harsh even the scorpions side-eye it.

## Paran: The Hood That Raised a Legend

Paran wasn't just a campsite. It became Ishmael's kingdom.

Geography Lesson: Stretching from Sinai to the edges of Canaan, Paran was the badlands—the kind of place where only the tough survived.

Ishmael's Glow-Up: The boy who nearly died of thirst becomes an archer (Gen 21:20). Not just good—elite. The kind of man who could hit a dove mid-flight and roast it before it hit the ground.

Twelve Tribes: His sons? Princes. His legacy? A nation. God's promise didn't just survive—it thrived in the soil of suffering.

## The Well's Secret History

Now, here's the kicker—that well? It wasn't done.

Years later, Isaac—the miracle child, the one who "replaced" Ishmael—finds himself in the same desert. And what does he do?

He redigs Hagar's well. (Gen 26:18)

Symbolism Alert: The Hebrew word "be'er" (well) is the same for both stories. God's provision isn't a one-time event. It's a generational lifeline.

Full Circle: The place where Hagar sobbed becomes the place Isaac thrives. The water that saved the outcast now feeds the chosen son.

**Why This Matters:** God doesn't just rescue. He reclaims. The very ground that witnessed Hagar's despair later witnesses Isaac's abundance.

The desert never forgot her. And neither did God.

This prayer teaches us:

1. God responds to **raw need**, not eloquence
2. Sometimes the miracle is **revealing what was there all along**
3. A mother's cry can **redirect history**

*Now pass the tissues and some Gatorade - we're all dehydrated from crying.*

# Chapter 19

# Lesson's from Hagar's Prayer

***O****R: WHY UGLY-SOBBING IN THE SHOWER MIGHT BE YOUR MOST POWERFUL PRAYER YET!*

*"She gave this name to the Lord who spoke to her: 'You are the God who sees me...'" (Genesis 16:13)*

### BIG IDEA: YOUR MESSIEST PRAYERS ARE GOD'S FAVORITES

Oh honey, can we just talk about this for a hot minute? Because Hagar absolutely *wrecked* everything I thought I knew about prayer.

You know how we've been taught that prayer should be this pristine, Sunday-best kind of thing? Like you need to shower, put on your good underwear, and maybe light a candle before you dare approach the Almighty? Yeah, Hagar took that rulebook and used it as kindling for her desert campfire.

This woman taught us that you don't need perfect words—you need a perfectly *honest* heart. And honey, when life decides to use you as a punching bag, honest hearts get *messy*.

Think about it—when Hagar screamed *"I can't do this!"* into that empty desert, she wasn't being dramatic. She was being *human*. She was that mom at the end of her rope, that woman who'd been pushed past every breaking point, and instead of prettying it up with theological jargon, she just... *broke*. Right there in the sand.

And you know what God did? He didn't hand her a tissues box and a "there, there." He rolled up His sleeves and got to work.

Hagar proved something revolutionary: God doesn't just tolerate our meltdowns—He actually *hunts down* hurting people like some kind of divine search-and-rescue team. While she's face-down in the dirt having what can only be described as the world's first recorded panic attack, God's already dispatched an angel. Not because she asked nicely. Not because she followed the proper prayer protocol. But because she was *real* about her pain.

And can we appreciate that she basically also used the *"bargaining with heaven while covered in snot"* prayer method? Because that's exactly what happened. No fancy posture, no eloquent words—just a woman ugly-crying her way into a miracle. She's literally the patron saint of shower cries and parking lot prayers.

The beautiful thing is, her prayer resume is absolutely unhinged if you think about it: one runaway attempt, one divine intervention, and exactly *zero* apologies for being dramatic. And God? He was apparently here for all of it.

*(Fun Bible Fact: Scholars believe Hagar's desert encounter was so significant that the location became a pilgrimage site. People literally traveled to visit the spot where a woman had the audacity to name God and live to tell about it.)*

## **SPIRITUAL TRUTHS (WITH EXTRA GLITTER AND A SIDE OF HOLY SASS)**

*A. Seen People Become Brave People (AKA The Ultimate Glow-Up)*

Okay sister, sit down because we need to talk about the moment that changed everything. When Hagar looked up from her desert breakdown and had the absolute audacity to name God "El Roi"—The God Who Sees—I'm pretty sure the angels did a collective double-take. Like, "Wait, did this slave girl just... name the Creator of the universe? And He's... okay with it?"

But here's what gets me every time: that moment when you realize Someone actually notices your pain? It's not just comforting—it's transformative. Like, life-altering, script-flipping, universe-rearranging kind of change. Because when you've spent your whole life being invisible, being overlooked, being treated like human furniture, and then the God of everything stops His day to see you? Baby, that rewrites your entire operating system.

Your "I'm worthless" narrative doesn't just get edited—it gets completely shredded and thrown in the cosmic trash can. Your survival mode, which has been running on fumes and pure stubbornness, suddenly gets this divine software update to thrival mode. Even those McDonald's hashbrowns you're stress-eating at 10 AM become holy ground because you realize God was there in that moment too, seeing your exhaustion, your overwhelm, your desperate need for something crispy and salty to get you through.

So here's your life hack, gorgeous: next time you catch yourself asking "God, where are You?" try flipping the script to "God, I know You see this hot mess—help!" Because the difference between those two prayers is the difference between begging for attention and knowing you already have it.

*B. Pain Unlocked Purpose (Or: How God Turns Your Trauma Into Someone Else's Treasure Map)*

Now listen, this next part is going to make you ugly-cry in the best possible way. Hagar technically wasn't "necessary" for Abraham's covenant story, right? Like, if we're being honest, God's promise to Abraham would've been just fine without her. She was the detour, the complication, the "what were they thinking?" subplot.

But here's where God shows off His divine sense of irony: He took this woman who was supposed to be a footnote and made her story absolutely essential. Not just for her own survival, but for every single person who's ever felt like a background character in their own life.

Think about it—her suffering, her rejection, her wilderness wandering became a lifeline for every overlooked woman throughout history. Every single mom who's ever felt abandoned. Every person who's ever thought "I'm just the side character in everyone else's main story." Every human being who's been cast off, written off, or counted out. Hagar's pain became their permission slip to believe they matter too.

Your worst chapters, sweet friend, might literally be someone else's survival guide. That depression you fought through? That's someone's proof they can make it. That toxic relationship you escaped? That's another woman's roadmap to freedom. That financial disaster you navigated? That's someone's blueprint for bouncing back.

*C. Wells Follow Weeping (The Most Beautiful Water Cycle You've Ever Heard)*

And can we just talk about this miraculous water source for a hot second? Because this isn't just a nice little Bible story—this is God's entire MO wrapped up in one beautiful, hope-inducing package.

That well that saved Hagar and Ishmael when they were literally dying of thirst? It didn't disappear after their miracle moment. Nope. Years later, when Isaac—the "chosen" son—finds himself in a famine, where does he go? He redigs Hagar's well. The same water source that saved the "outcast" becomes the lifeline for the "blessed" son.

And you know what that whispers to us today? "Your tear-soaked ground might be the next miracle site." Those places where you've cried until you couldn't breathe, where you've prayed until your voice gave out, where you've felt most abandoned—those might be exactly the spots where God's preparing springs of hope for the next person who stumbles into that desert.

Here's your theological mic drop moment: the Hebrew word "be'er" means both "well" and "to explain." God doesn't just give us water in our drought—He helps us understand why we had to walk through the dry season in the first place. The well and the wisdom come as a package deal.

So every tear you've cried? It's not wasted water. It's irrigation for someone else's miracle garden.

## MY HOT MESS TESTIMONY

Okay, sweet friend, buckle up because I'm about to get *real* vulnerable with you. Like, "why am I telling strangers my business" level of real. But sometimes God uses our messiest stories to help other people feel less alone, so here we go.

Two years ago, I became absolutely *fixated* on Hagar. Like, obsessed to the point where my friends probably wanted to stage an intervention. "Girl, we get it, you love the desert lady, but can we talk about literally anything else?" But I couldn't let it go because something about her story was eating at me from the inside out.

See, I knew what it felt like to be unseen. I'd lived through epic childhood abuse—the kind that leaves invisible scars and makes you wonder if you're even worth the air you breathe.

So when I read about Hagar running away from Sarah's cruelty, I got it. But what I *couldn't* understand, what kept me up at night picking at this story like a scab, was why she went back. And more than that, why God made her story important at all.

I mean, think about it—God's promise to Abraham would've been just fine without Hagar's drama, right? She wasn't essential to the covenant. She was the complication, the detour, the "oops" in the grand plan. So why did God bother with her?

I prayed so many snotty-nose prayers in the shower about this. Picture me, standing under scalding water, ugly-crying and demanding answers from the Almighty like I had any right to question His storytelling choices. "Why her, God? Why make her matter when she didn't have to?"

Then one completely ordinary Tuesday, I'm sitting in McDonald's—because apparently that's where I have all my spiritual breakthroughs now—getting my usual coffee and hashbrown (don't judge my breakfast choices), and I'm rereading Hagar's story for the millionth time when God just... *nudged* me.

Not audibly, but you know that feeling when a thought drops into your brain that's so clearly not your own? That happened. And the question was simple: *"What did you want when you were going through all that stuff?"*

My first answer was easy: "I wanted it to stop." But then came the follow-up: *"But before that, what did you want?"*

And that's when it hit me like a freight train made of holy revelation and McDonald's grease: *To be seen.*

*"Why do you think she called Me 'The God Who Sees'?"*

Friend, when I tell you a thousand light bulbs switched on in that moment, I'm not being dramatic. I just started *sobbing* right there in the McCafé, probably scaring the teenage employees and definitely making the other customers question my mental stability. But I couldn't help it because I finally understood.

See I guess i just thought El Roi was just a nice pretty name she came up with. But she meant it. She meant, he saw her, he saw her in her pain, in her agony, in her mess.

I remembered being seven or eight years old, walking into school with bruising around my eyes and nose because my mother had broken my nose the night before. I remember trying to cover it with my hair, walking with my head down, hoping nobody would notice.

But my teacher—God bless her—she noticed. At the end of class, she gently sat me down and asked what happened. And for the first time in my little life, I told someone the truth. I just spilled and cried and fear set in as it was time to go back home.

She hugged me. Actually *hugged* me. She saw me through it all, she saw my pain and didn't just ignore it, like everyone else in my life did.

Then she called family services, and for a brief, shining moment, I thought someone was finally going to save me, see me. Maybe someone will call my dad and he will come for me. Of course, back then they never really talked to the kids—just the parents—and I got the beating of my life for "telling lies" about my family. I was transferred to a different school, and I never saw that teacher again.

But you know what? That moment when she *saw* me, when she cared enough to ask and then to act—that moment kept me alive. I'd spend so many nights in the shower after that, crying through nightmares and panic attacks, praying desperately for my dad to come get me because somehow I'd convinced myself that if I could just get him to *see* me, really see me, he'd take me away from all of it.

He never did. The abuse didn't stop.

But what I didn't know then—what I was too young and too traumatized to understand—was that God was with me every single day. Every nightmare that somehow turned into peaceful sleep, every panic attack that eventually calmed, every moment I found the strength to keep going when everything in me wanted to give up—that was Him, cupping water from His well for my parched little soul.

That teacher saw me for maybe ten minutes of my entire childhood, but it was enough to show me that I was worth seeing. That my pain mattered. That *I* mattered.

And that's exactly what God did for Hagar. In a world where she was invisible, disposable, forgettable—He stopped everything to see her. Not because she was necessary to His plan, but because she was precious to His heart.

Hagar taught me that God doesn't just watch our pain from a distance like some cosmic voyeur. He leans in. He gets close. He's cupping living water for our souls when we're dying of thirst, even when we don't realize that's what's happening.

## PRAYER PRACTICE: HAGAR-IFY YOUR PRAYER LIFE

Try This:

The "Name It & Claim It" Remix

Next meltdown, name God by what you *need*: *"El Roi—You SEE this panic attack!"*

Scribble Your Seven-Word Scream

Write your rawest prayer in lipstick/chapstick on your mirror: *"Don't let me drown today." "You promised better than this. Remember, Help me understand and see it through"* (Isaiah 62:6-7)

Well Redigging

Return to places where God showed up before. Text an old friend: *"Remember when we prayed through that crisis? God's still that faithful."*

## BLESSING FOR THE UNSEEN ONES (THIS IS WHERE WE UGLY-CRY TOGETHER)

Oh sweet, beautiful, battle-scarred sister—can we just sit here together for a minute? Because if Hagar's story has taught us anything, it's that you and I? We've never been as invisible as we thought we were.

Listen to me carefully, because I need you to hear this in your bones: your pain has a *witness*. Not just any witness—the kind of witness that matters.

The kind that sees every tear you've tried to hide, every bruise you've covered with makeup, every night you've cried yourself to sleep thinking nobody cares. Your suffering isn't happening in a vacuum. It's not meaningless background noise in the cosmic symphony. Someone is watching, Someone is taking notes, and Someone is absolutely *furious* on your behalf and making victory plans.

And your survival? Oh honey, your survival has *meaning* that stretches far beyond what you can see right now.

Every day you chose to keep breathing when your lungs felt like they were filled with concrete, every morning you got out of bed when staying under the covers seemed like the only safe option, every single moment you refused to let your story end in the darkness—that's not just personal victory. That's a roadmap for someone else who's walking through their own desert right now, wondering if they're going to make it.

You know what gets me every time I think about Hagar? She thought she was just running away from an impossible situation. She had no idea she was running straight into her destiny. She had no clue that her breakdown in the desert would become breakthrough for generations of women who needed to know that God sees the overlooked, the discarded, the forgotten.

Your *"not enough"* story? That thing you're so ashamed of, that thing you think disqualifies you from God's love, that thing that makes you feel like damaged goods?

God looks at that and says *"just watch Me."* He takes your broken pieces and turns them into stained glass windows that catch the light in ways that perfect, unbroken glass never could.

So here's what I want you to do, beautiful one. The next time you're overwhelmed, the next time you feel invisible, the next time the weight of your story feels too heavy to carry—borrow Hagar's prayer. It's simple, it's raw, and it works:

*"SEE ME. FIGHT FOR ME. REMEMBER ME."*

That's it. No fancy theological language. No perfect posture required. Just three desperate declarations from a heart that knows its worth, even when the world tries to convince it otherwise.

*"SEE ME"*—because you're tired of being overlooked, tired of being treated like you don't matter, tired of feeling invisible in your own life.

*"FIGHT FOR ME"*—because sometimes you're too exhausted to fight for yourself, and you need Someone with bigger fists and better aim to step into the ring on your behalf.

*"REMEMBER ME"*—because in a world that's quick to forget, you need to know that your story is written in permanent ink in the heart of God.

Because here's the thing that makes me want to happy-dance in grocery store aisles: the same God who tracked down a slave girl in the desert, who stopped everything He was doing to tend to her broken heart, who gave her a new name and a new story—that God is already turning His head toward *your* wilderness. He's already packing His bags, rolling up His sleeves, getting ready to show up in ways that will leave you ugly-crying with gratitude.

Your desert isn't a punishment. It's a meeting place. Your breakdown isn't the end of your story—it's the setup for your comeback. And your tears? They're not signs of weakness. They're prayers in liquid form, and every single one of them is being collected in heaven's bottles like precious perfume.

So go ahead, sweet friend. Pray messy. Cry hard. Scream into your pillow if you need to. God's not intimidated by your intensity—He's attracted to your authenticity.

He's not waiting for you to get your act together before He shows up. He's already there, sitting in the mess with you, ready to turn your wilderness into a wellspring.

You are seen. You are known. You are loved beyond measure.

And if that doesn't make you want to ugly-cry into your coffee with gratitude, I don't know what will.

*(Now excuse me while I go practice what I preach and have my own snotty prayer session. Because sometimes the best theology happens in the shower, and I've got some serious thanking to do.)*

# ANNA THE PROPHETESS

*"She never left the temple but worshiped night and day, fasting and praying."*
*— Luke 2:37 (NIV)*

# ANNA
## THE PROPHETESS

# Chapter 20

# The Story of Anna

## "*Or: The OG TikTok Prophetess (But Without the Dance Moves)*"

*"She never left the temple but worshiped night and day, fasting and praying." — Luke 2:37 (NIV)*

Picture this: an 84-year-old woman, wrapped in prayer shawls like a holy burrito, has basically turned the Jerusalem Temple into her Airbnb for six decades. She's seen more sunrises than a rooster with insomnia, outlasted more high priests than contestants on a biblical game show, and her knees? They've got permanent grooves from those stone floors. Meet Anna — the woman who made waiting an Olympic sport.

But every epic tale has a beginning. Back when Anna was young (think biblical Taylor Swift era, but with more sandals), she hailed from the tribe of Asher. Now, Asher was the "blink and you'll miss them" tribe of Israel. The one Jacob prophesied would "yield royal dainties" (Genesis 49:20). Translation: *"You guys will be known for snacks."* Basically, if the other tribes were lions and warriors, Asher was the cousin who brought the dessert platter to family reunions. Little did they know, Anna herself would become the "royal dainty" — sweet, enduring, and impossible to forget.

Anna probably grew up in a sleepy Galilean village, hearing stories about her tribe's lost glory. She might've giggled with her sisters while helping knead dough for olive cakes, eyes wide as traveling rabbis came through with tales of prophets and kings. Like every Jewish girl, she dreamed of a future that included a husband, children, Sabbath meals under fig trees, and a few decades of complaining together about the neighbors' noisy goats.

Marriage came early, as it usually did back then. For seven years, Anna had her dream: a husband, a home, maybe plans for a family. We don't know his name, but we know he must have been precious to her — because when widowhood hit, it shattered her world. One day, she was planning life; the next, she was planning survival. Widowhood in first-century wasn't romantic. It meant vulnerability. It meant whispers. It meant living at the mercy of your extended family or the charity of your community.

Most women in Anna's shoes had three options:

**Option A:** Remarry quickly, because society treated women like milk cartons with an expiration date.

**Option B:** Move back in with relatives and spend the next 50 years babysitting cousins' kids while mediating family goat disputes.

**Option C:** Fade into obscurity, remembered only as "so-and-so's widow."

But Anna? She went with **Option D: Become a Temple legend.**

Instead of shrinking, she showed up. Instead of bitterness, she leaned into prayer. She packed her shawls, marched into the Temple courts, and basically said, *"Fine. If life won't give me a home, I'll make God's house my home."*

And there she stayed. Through Roman soldiers clanging their swords in the streets. Through corrupt high priests cozying up to Herod. Through Passovers packed shoulder-to-shoulder with pilgrims. She fasted. She prayed. She worshiped. And somewhere along the way, people stopped calling her "the widow Anna" and started whispering "the prophetess."

Think about it: while others were chasing comfort, Anna was chasing God. She waited decades — not for a husband, not for status, not for retirement — but for a Messiah. Her life became one long countdown, a drumbeat of hope that never gave out.

By the time she reached her 80s, Anna wasn't just another old woman in the Temple. She was a fixture. A spiritual landmark. The one who had seen it all, prayed it all, and was still there every morning when the gates opened, shawl wrapped tight, ready to watch for the One she knew would come.

### Temple Life: The Ultimate Spiritual Boot Camp

So, let's talk about Anna's "night and day" worship gig. On paper, it sounds peaceful, right? Like a serene retreat center with harp music, candlelight, and maybe a cozy beanbag chair in the corner. Wrong. Anna's prayer fortress was the Jerusalem Temple — ancient Israel's equivalent of Grand Central Station, except swap the pigeons for doves destined for sacrifice, add nonstop incense, and multiply the chaos by a thousand.

Every single day was a sensory overload:

**Dawn:** The priests kicked things off with the morning sacrifice. Cue the trumpet fanfare that could've given any marching band halftime show a run for its money. Anna probably muttered, "Here we go again," while rubbing the sleep out of her eyes.

**Morning Rush Hour:** Pilgrims poured in like Black Friday shoppers, except they were fighting for atonement instead of flat-screen TVs.

**Midday Madness:** Tourists flocked from across the empire, gawking at Herod's architectural flex — polished marble, massive courtyards, gold glittering in the sunlight. Imagine ancient Instagram influencers but with scrolls and sandals: "#TempleGoals."

**Evening Sacrifice:** Another round of trumpet blasts, chanting priests, and a river of animals meeting their destiny.

**Night:** The sane people went home. Anna? She was just clocking in for her graveyard shift of prayer.

And here's a fun Bible fact: Anna's hangout spot was the Court of Women. Misleading name, because everyone who wasn't a priest gathered there. It was basically the Temple's food court slash town square. For six decades, Anna had a front-row seat to every major feast, festival, and controversy. She knew more Temple drama than TMZ knows celebrity scandals.

Imagine waiting for something for sixty years. That's longer than:

The Beatles' entire existence (1960-1970), Most people's careers, The time between "I'll be there in 5 minutes" and actually arriving

But Anna wasn't twiddling her thumbs. She was training. Every fast was conditioning. Every whispered psalm was target practice. Every cold night spent curled on stone floors was spiritual weightlifting. By the time she hit her 80s, Anna wasn't just an old widow. She was basically a Navy SEAL of prayer.

Other widows spent their golden years knitting prayer shawls and complaining about olive oil prices. Anna turned her widowhood into boot camp. Her grief became her grind. Her waiting became her weapon.

And then, finally, it happened.

Picture Anna at 84, creaky joints, prayer shawl wrapped like armor, probably scolding the priests under her breath: "Light the incense properly this time, for heaven's sake." Another ordinary Tuesday in Temple life... until suddenly—

**Enter stage right: Mary, Joseph, and Baby Jesus.**

Luke tells us Simeon, another longtime waiter, got there first. He scooped up baby Jesus and started his prophetic happy dance. But Anna? Please. Simeon was the JV team. She had been on varsity for six decades. Her prophet-senses tingled like Spiderman's. She shuffled closer, peered over Simeon's shoulder, and—BOOM. Divine download.

Luke 2:38 says she "gave thanks to God and spoke about the child to all who were looking forward to the redemption of Jerusalem." That's the short version. The real version? Picture Anna going full-on PR mode:

"EXCUSE ME! YOU THERE WITH THE TRAVELING SANDALS—YES, YOU. PUT DOWN YOUR PIGEON AND LISTEN. See this baby? THIS is the One. The Messiah. The redemption of Jerusalem! Do you know how long I've been waiting here? SIXTY YEARS. SIXTY. YEARS. And let me tell you—every fast, every stone floor, every sunrise I thought might be my last—it was worth it."

Anna didn't just recognize Jesus. She became His hype woman. His heavenly press secretary. The Temple courts turned into the first-ever Christian broadcasting network, powered by one old widow who refused to quit.

Because when everyone else forgot the promises, Anna stayed. When everyone else moved on, Anna kept her eyes open. And when God finally showed up wrapped in swaddling clothes, Anna was ready to shout it from the rooftops.

Anna didn't just recognize Jesus—she became heaven's press secretary. While most people were wondering who this random baby was, Anna was already running a one-woman PR campaign for the Messiah. She turned the Temple courts into the first Christian broadcasting network.

**Here's what makes Anna legendary:**

- She chose **devotion over despair**
- She turned **waiting into worship**
- She made **preparation her profession**
- She transformed **loss into legacy**

The woman from the "forgotten" tribe became unforgettable. From Asher—the tribe that rarely gets mentioned in biblical hall-of-fame lists—came the prophetess who announced the Messiah to Jerusalem. Talk about God's sense of poetic justice.

Little did Anna know that her decades of predawn prayer meetings, her marathon fasting sessions, and her stubborn refusal to give up were about to hit spiritual ROI beyond her wildest dreams. She didn't just witness history—she announced it. Next chapter? We're diving into Anna's prayer playbook—because when you've spent 60 years perfecting the art of talking to God, you've earned the right to teach us how to pray like the Temple depends on it.

**Historical Deep Dive Nuggets:**

The Tribe of Asher was known for producing olive oil and being prosperous but often politically invisible—fitting that their daughter would be spiritually visible when it mattered most

Temple life for women was restricted to the Court of Women, but Anna maximized her access like a spiritual VIP member

Prophetic ministry for women was rare but not unprecedented—Anna joins the ranks of Deborah, Hulda, and Miriam

The "redemption of Jerusalem" Anna spoke about wasn't just spiritual—it was political, social, and cosmic. She was announcing the ultimate game-changer.

Historical Nugget: Ancient Jewish tradition says Anna was one of the "seven prophetesses" of Israel (likely why Luke name-drops her alongside Simeon).

Sassy Translation: Her name means "grace"—fitting, since she extended grace to a nation that forgot widows faster than last year's Passover leftovers.

(Now excuse me while I go apologize to my prayer life for complaining about "long" 10-minute devotionals.)

# Chapter 21

# Anna's Temple Prayer Life

**"O**R: HOW TO TURN THE TEMPLE INTO YOUR PERSONAL HOTLINE TO HEAVEN"

> *"She never left the temple but worshipped night and day, fasting and praying."* — Luke 2:37 (NIV)

After sixty-plus years of widowhood, watching Jerusalem's spiritual temperature drop faster than a stone tablet, Anna was DONE with polite, surface-level religion. She'd seen priests phone it in, pilgrims treat the Temple like a spiritual tourist trap, and an entire generation lose hope that God still remembered His promises. Meanwhile, she's been camping out in God's house longer than some people live, watching the clock tick toward eternity like the world's most patient bouncer waiting for the VIP to show up.

> *"Is not this the kind of fasting I have chosen: to loose the chains of injustice and untie the cords of the yoke, to set the oppressed free and break every yoke?"* — Isaiah 58:6

Anna wasn't just skipping meals—she was loosing chains that had bound Israel's hope for centuries.

What finally broke her into this legendary prayer marathon? Probably the realisation that if she didn't hold down the prayer fort, who would?

You're surrounded by religious professionals who've turned worship into a 9-to-5 job, pilgrims who pray like they're ordering fast food, and a nation that's forgotten what it feels like to actually *expect* God to show up. Someone had to keep the spiritual lights on—and Anna decided that someone was her.

Just like Esther facing the crisis of her people's extinction, Anna saw the spiritual crisis of her nation and chose radical action over comfortable silence.

This wasn't some polite "bless this food and keep us safe" dinner prayer—this was spiritual warfare disguised as worship. Anna had turned intercession into an extreme sport.

The Greek word for "worshipped" (*latreuo*) doesn't just mean "attended church." It means sacred service—the kind reserved for priests performing holy duties. Anna wasn't just praying; she was functioning as Jerusalem's unofficial priest, standing in the gap between heaven and earth like a spiritual air traffic controller.

> *"Therefore he is able to save completely those who come to God through him, because he always lives to intercede for them."* — Hebrews 7:25

Anna was modeling Christ's own ministry before He even arrived—constant intercession for God's people.

"Fasting and praying" (*nēsteiais kai deēsesin*) literally means "abstinences and petitions." But here's what we miss in translation: Anna wasn't just skipping meals—she was creating space. In Jewish culture, fasting wasn't about weight loss; it was about making room for God to move by removing everything that might compete for your attention.

The phrase "night and day" (*nykta kai hēmeran*) is the same construction used to describe God's constant care in other passages. Anna had synchronized her prayer rhythm with heaven's heartbeat. She wasn't just praying occasionally—she was breathing prayers.

> *"He will call on me, and I will answer him; I will be with him in trouble, I will deliver him and honor him."* — **Psalm 91:15**

### Let's break down what Anna's intercession probably looked like:

Dawn Prayers (The "Good Morning, God" Sessions):

Thanksgiving for surviving another night
*"The steadfast love of the Lord never ceases; his mercies are new every morning"* — Lamentations 3:22-23
Intercession for Jerusalem's redemption (her greatest obsession)
Prophetic listening (tuning her spiritual antenna)

Midday Prayers (The "Divine Check-In"):

Worship during the daily sacrifices
*"Let my prayer be set before you like incense; may the lifting up of my hands be like the evening sacrifice"* — Psalm 141:2

Petition for the Messiah's coming (her daily "Are we there yet?")

Blessing the pilgrims and priests (unauthorized pastoral care)

Evening Prayers (The "Don't Let Me Down Now, God"):

Confession for the nation's sins
*"If my people, who are called by my name, will humble themselves and pray and seek my face and turn from their wicked ways, then I will hear from heaven"* — 2 Chronicles 7:14

Protection prayers for Jerusalem (ancient homeland security)

Promise-claiming based on Scripture (spiritual legal proceedings)

Midnight Prayers (The "While Everyone Else Sleeps" Shift):

Warfare praying against spiritual darkness
*"At midnight I rise to give you thanks"* — Psalm 119:62

Prophetic intercession for future generations (long-term investment)

Deep communion with God (the mystical hours)

When other widows probably said, "Anna, don't you think you're being a bit... extra? Maybe get a hobby?"

Anna's likely response: "Honey, I AM the hobby. I'm professionally waiting for the Messiah, and business is about to BOOM."

"But when you pray, go into your room, close the door and pray to your Father, who is unseen. Then your Father, who sees what is done in secret, will reward you." — Matthew 6:6

Anna took this literally—the Temple became her room, and her reward was seeing the Messiah.

When priests might have suggested, "Perhaps you could pray from home like other women?"

Anna's probable comeback: "Listen, boys, I've been here longer than most of your careers. I've earned squatter's rights in the Court of Women, and I'm not moving until the One I'm waiting for shows up."

### The Persistent Widow: "

*And will not God bring about justice for his chosen ones, who cry out to him day and night? Will he keep putting them off?"* — Luke 18:7

### Hannah's Temple Vigil:

*"As she kept on praying to the Lord, Eli observed her mouth. Hannah was praying in her heart, and her lips were moving but her voice was not heard."* — 1 Samuel 1:12-13

The cultural context here is HUGE. Women weren't supposed to be religious leaders, widows were expected to fade into the background, and 84-year-olds definitely weren't supposed to be pulling all-nighters in the Temple. Anna was basically staging a holy rebellion disguised as devotion.

Then God pulled off the ultimate divine plot twist. After sixty years of Anna's relentless intercession, He didn't just answer her prayers—He delivered them personally.

## What Anna's story teaches us about God's timing:

Abraham waited 25 years for Isaac — Anna waited 60+ years for the Messiah Moses spent 40 years in the wilderness — Anna spent 60+ years in the Temple David waited 15 years between anointing and coronation — Anna waited 60+ years between calling and confirmation.

While the high priests were busy with their religious bureaucracy, while the scribes were debating theological fine print, while the Pharisees were polishing their spiritual résumés, God chose to reveal His Son to an 84-year-old widow who'd been camping in His house like a holy homeless person.

The moment Anna saw Baby Jesus wasn't just answered prayer—it was divine vindication. God was essentially saying, "You know that woman who's been praying here longer than anyone can remember? SHE gets the exclusive preview of salvation."

*"And we know that in all things God works for the good of those who love him, who have been called according to his purpose."* — Romans 8:28

She immediately became Jerusalem's first evangelist, spreading the news about Jesus to everyone "who were looking forward to the redemption of Jerusalem" (Luke 2:38). After decades of asking God for the Messiah, she spent her remaining years telling everyone He'd arrived.

*"How beautiful on the mountains are the feet of those who bring good news, who proclaim peace, who bring good tidings, who proclaim salvation, who say to Zion, 'Your God reigns!'"* — Isaiah 52:7

Here's what Anna understood that we often miss: Prayer isn't just asking God for stuff—it's participating in His plan. Every night she spent on cold Temple stones, every meal she skipped to pray instead, every moment she chose intercession over comfort was preparing the spiritual atmosphere for the Messiah's arrival.

Anna's prayer life was prophetic preparation. She wasn't just waiting for Jesus to show up; she was creating the conditions for His recognition. When the Son of God walked into the Temple, there was already a woman there who'd been talking to His Father about Him for sixty years.

Which brings us to the revolutionary truth Anna discovered: The reward for faithful prayer isn't just answered prayer—it's transformation into the kind of person who can recognize God's answers when they arrive. Anna didn't just pray for the Messiah; her decades of intercession shaped her into someone who could spot Him in a crowd.

*"Let us then approach God's throne of grace with confidence, so that we may receive mercy and find grace to help us in our time of need."* — Hebrews 4:16

## Deep Research Nuggets:

- Temple prayer times followed Jewish *shacharit* (morning), *mincha* (afternoon), and *maariv* (evening) patterns—Anna was doing 24/7 coverage

- Women's religious roles were limited, but prophetic ministry was recognized—Anna found her lane and dominated it
- Intercession theology in Judaism saw prayer as literally standing between God's justice and human need—Anna was a professional mediator
- The "redemption of Jerusalem" (*lytrōsin Ierousalēm*) wasn't just spiritual—it was political, economic, and social liberation rolled into one cosmic package

# Chapter 22

# Lessons from Anna's Prayer

**"OR: HOW TO WAIT ON GOD WITHOUT LOSING YOUR HOLY MIND"**

*"She who goes out weeping, carrying seed to sow, will return with songs of joy, carrying sheaves with her."* — Psalm 126:6 (NIV) (AKA Anna's theme verse before it was cool)

Anna teaches us that God's delay ≠ God's denial, and that holy persistence has a way of turning ordinary grandmas into prophets. At 84 years old, with knees creakier than the Temple doors, she proved that faith isn't a sprint. It's a marathon where the finish line is "until Jesus shows up." And spoiler alert: He did.

But how do we get there without losing our minds (or our patience)? Anna leaves us a trail of breadcrumbs.

## Truth #1: The Tortoise Beats the Hare Every Time

Anna knew what so many biblical heroes had to learn the hard way: God's timing is never rushed, but it's always right. Moses spent forty years chasing sheep before leading people (Exodus 3). Joseph endured prison jumpsuits before donning royal robes (Genesis 41). David hid out in caves for thirteen years before getting his crown (1 Samuel 16 – 2 Samuel 5).

Meanwhile, we treat prayer like Uber Eats—expecting God to deliver in thirty minutes or less or the miracle's free. Anna treated prayer like Thanksgiving dinner: slow-cooked, perfectly seasoned, and absolutely worth the wait.

## Truth #2: Location, Location, Devotion

Elijah prayed by a brook, then in a palace, then under a broom tree. Jonah prayed from fish guts (ew). Peter prayed walking on water, then sinking under it. But Anna? She picked one spot and stayed.

She turned the Court of Women into her war room. Same place, same prayers, day after day, decade after decade. And here's the hilarious twist: the Temple probably had worse Wi-Fi than your local coffee shop, yet Anna never ghosted God.

Her message is simple: you don't need a perfect place to meet God. You just need a consistent one.

## Truth #3: Senior Discounts Apply to Spiritual Breakthroughs

At an age when most modern believers are complaining about worship music being "too loud" or telling kids to "get off their spiritual lawn," Anna was out here birthing revival. She was a spiritual grandma delivering triplets: persistence, prophecy, and praise.

Fun Bible fact: Anna's name means *grace* — which fits, because she extended grace to a generation that moved slower than dial-up internet. Her tribe, Asher, means *happy* — and happiness is exactly what bubbled out of her the day she finally saw the Messiah.

### PRAYER PRACTICE: THE "ANNA LITE" CHALLENGE

Now, let's be real: most of us don't have sixty years to camp out in church pews without snacks. So here's a modern take — baby steps toward Anna-level faith.

**Week 1 – Basic Training:** Pray five minutes daily without touching your phone (Luke 18:1). Pick a prayer spot and stick with it. Name your "Messiah wait" — that one thing you're still believing God for.

**Week 2 – Level Up:** Fast one comfort (coffee, Netflix, doomscrolling). Add intercession: pray daily for one other person (1 Timothy 2:1).

**Week 3 – Hardcore Mode:** Add thanksgiving before answers show up (1 Thessalonians 5:18). Memorize Anna's mantra: *"God's got this even when I don't have a clue."*

**Week 4 – Prophet Status:** Ask God for eyes to see His work (Psalm 119:18). Tell someone about your prayer journey.

Congratulations, you just became a modern evangelist (Matthew 28:19).

Warning: side effects may include answered prayers, actual peace, and annoying your friends by talking about Jesus all the time (like Anna did).

**THE TAKEAWAY**

Anna proves this simple equation: Ordinary people + extraordinary persistence = history makers. God tracks every prayer mile you've ever prayed, even the ones you forgot. Your waiting room isn't wasted time — it's training ground.

She's basically the biblical version of that grandma who prays fifty years for her wayward son... and one day he walks into a revival meeting. Coincidence? Nope. Faithful sowing.

Anna whispers to our impatient souls: *"What if your 'delay' is actually God's development?"* While we stress over timetables, heaven is marinating the miracle.

Remember: Anna waited 22,000 days to see her Messiah. Your 22 days? That's just the warm-up.

Sweet sister, may you develop Anna's holy stubbornness — the kind that outlasts every "not yet" until it becomes "now."

May you gain her prophetic joy — where you can't stop talking about Jesus like He's the best gossip at the heavenly water cooler.

May you inherit her senior-citizen superpowers — where age, or waiting, or disappointment just means you've got more testimonies than tears.

Go forth and pray like the Wi-Fi's out and God is your only signal. Because Anna proved that persistent prayers download miracles so big, they take decades to buffer.

And when they finally arrive? Oh, sister, it will be worth every stone floor, every sleepless night, every whispered "How long, Lord?"

Because the God who showed up for Anna will show up for you.

# SYROPHOENICIAN WOMAN

*"Then Jesus said to her, 'Woman, you have great faith! Your request is granted.' And her daughter was healed at that moment."*
— Matthew 15:28

# SYROPHOENICIAN WOMAN

# Chapter 23

# The Story of the Syrophoenician Woman

## O R: HOW A PAGAN MOM CRASHED JESUS' JEWISH-ONLY PARTY AND CHANGED HISTORY

*"Then Jesus said to her, 'Woman, you have great faith! Your request is granted.' And her daughter was healed at that moment."*
— Matthew 15:28

A desperate mother pacing the dusty streets of Tyre, clutching her shawl tight against the salty Mediterranean wind. Back home, her daughter — her baby, her heart — is writhing in torment, possessed by something dark and unspeakable. This isn't your typical soccer mom stress about late homework or missing shin guards. No, this is ancient-world, life-or-death, "I've tried everything and my baby is slipping away" desperation.

Meet the Syrophoenician woman — the ultimate outsider, the mama bear who gate-crashed Jesus' ministry and proved that a mother's cry can bulldoze every cultural boundary, every religious rule, every social stigma.

But before we see her storm heaven's gates, we need to set the scene properly.

Welcome to Tyre: Ancient World's Vegas (But With More Fish and Fewer Showgirls).
Tyre wasn't exactly the suburbs. Picture a bustling port city where:

**Phoenician merchants** hawked purple dye worth more than your house.

**Greek philosophers** debated the meaning of life over wine that could knock you sideways

**Roman soldiers** strutted around like they owned the place (because they kinda did)

**Local pagans** worshipped Baal, Astarte, and whatever god seemed most likely to make it rain

Our girl lived smack in the middle of this cultural melting pot, about 30 miles north of Israel. Think of it as the ancient equivalent of living in a diverse city where your neighbors speak five different languages, worship different gods, and nobody agrees on the proper way to season fish.

The religious landscape? Let's just say if you threw a stone in Tyre, you'd hit three different temples, two fortune tellers, and a guy selling "blessed" amulets that probably came from a back-alley pottery shop.

What did our heroine's typical Tuesday look like before her world imploded?

Wake up to the sound of ships docking.
Haggle for bread that wasn't fossilized.
Dodge Roman tax collectors (ancient IRS).
Whisper neighborhood gossip: "Did you hear Marcus came home drunk again?"
Pray to whichever god might be listening that day.
Collapse in bed, wondering if tomorrow's hustle would be kinder

## Her biggest worries were probably:

Whether the fish vendor was cheating her on weight (*"This mackerel looks suspicious, Marcus!"*)

If her daughter would marry well despite not being Jewish (limited dating pool in the ancient world)

Whether the latest Roman tax increase would bankrupt them

Syrophoenician women actually had more legal rights than their Jewish counterparts—they could own property, run businesses, and speak in public. Our girl was already operating in "boss lady" mode before she even met Jesus.

Then life decided to use our mama as a spiritual punching bag.

Her daughter—her precious, beautiful, irreplaceable little girl—started exhibiting signs that made every parent's blood run cold. We're not talking about teenage attitude or back-talk. This was full-blown demonic possession:

- **Violent outbursts** that required multiple adults to restrain her
- **Voices speaking** that weren't her own (and saying things that would make a sailor blush)
- **Superhuman strength** during episodes (think *The Exorcist* but without special effects)
- **Complete personality changes** where her sweet daughter became unrecognizable

*Modern equivalent:* Imagine your kid suddenly needing psychiatric holds, speaking in languages they've never learned, and exhibiting strength that defies medical explanation. Every parent's worst nightmare.

The cultural context makes this even more heartbreaking. In the ancient world:

- **Mental illness** was often seen as divine punishment
- **Demon possession** meant your family was cursed
- **Social isolation** was inevitable—who wants to hang around a "cursed" family?

Our mama tried EVERYTHING:

1. **Local priests** performed expensive rituals (*"That'll be 50 denarii, and maybe Baal will consider helping"*)

2. **Greek physicians** prescribed herbs that did absolutely nothing (*"Try this root. If she dies, we'll refund half your payment"*)
3. **Fortune tellers** gave conflicting advice (*"The stars say... uh... keep trying?"*)
4. **Temple prostitutes** probably suggested appeasing Astarte with more offerings (*"The goddess demands gold jewelry. Coincidentally, we accept donations"*)

Nothing worked. Every day, her daughter got worse. Every night, our mama fell asleep to the sound of her child's torment.

Then the gossip mill started buzzing about a Jewish rabbi named Jesus who was supposedly healing people. Not just headaches or broken bones—we're talking blind people seeing, dead people walking, and demons fleeing like their pants were on fire.

*"But he's Jewish,"* her neighbors whispered. *"He doesn't heal our kind."*

## Here's where our girl proves she's got titanium ovaries.

Instead of accepting *"He's not for us,"* she did what desperate mothers have done throughout history—she said *"Watch me."*

The journey from Tyre to wherever Jesus was, took planning:

Who would watch her daughter? (Probably multiple strong relatives)
How long could she be gone? (However long it took)
What if Jesus refused? (Cross that bridge when she got there)

Most importantly: "What if this doesn't work?"

Her answer? "Then at least I'll know I tried everything."

Before we get to the main event, let's appreciate the sheer audacity of what our mama was attempting. She wasn't just crossing geographical boundaries—she was obliterating cultural ones.

**The Jewish-Gentile Relationship Status:** *It's Complicated*

Jews considered Gentiles spiritually unclean (touching them required ritual purification)
Gentiles often resented Jewish exclusivity (*"Oh, so you're God's chosen people? How convenient"*)
Intermarriage was forbidden (Romeo and Juliet had nothing on Jewish-Gentile romance drama)
Religious interactions were minimal at best, hostile at worst

A Gentile woman approaching a Jewish rabbi was like a vegetarian showing up to a barbecue competition—technically possible, but definitely awkward.

**Add then gender dynamics:**

Women didn't approach male teachers uninvited
Mothers were expected to handle family crises quietly
Foreigners knew their place and it wasn't bothering important Jewish men

Our girl was about to violate every social norm simultaneously. It's like she decided to streak through a conservative church service while shouting political opinions—bold, shocking, and guaranteed to get attention.

## THE FAITH THAT DEFIED LOGIC

Here's what gets me every time I read this story: She had no theological training. No Bible study background. No Christian upbringing. She was just a pagan mom who'd heard rumors about a Jewish healer and thought, *"Worth a shot."*

Her prayer life probably consisted of:

Throwing coins in temple fountains (*"Please, Astarte, help my daughter"*)
Lighting incense to multiple gods (*"I'll take help from anyone at this point"*)
Muttering desperate pleas to whatever deity might be listening (*"If you're real, do something!"*)

Yet somehow, this theologically untrained, culturally excluded, socially inappropriate woman had more faith than most of Jesus' trained disciples.

*Fun Bible Fact:* The Greek word for her ethnicity, "Syrophoenician," appears only twice in the New Testament—both times referring to her. She's literally a category of one, the ultimate outsider who became an insider through sheer audacious faith.

The Syrophoenician Woman proves three revolutionary truths:

## Desperation + Faith = Miracles

She didn't need perfect theology—just perfect love for her daughter
Her prayer wasn't eloquent—it was effective

## God's Love Crosses Every Boundary

Race? Irrelevant
Religion? Negotiable
Social status? God doesn't check your credentials

## Mama Bear Faith Moves Mountains

Never underestimate a mother fighting for her child
Sometimes the most powerful prayers come from the most unexpected people

Little did our heroine know that her journey to find Jesus would result in one of the most theologically loaded conversations in the Gospels. She was about to engage in a verbal sparring match with the Son of God—and somehow manage to change His mind (or at least reveal His heart).

Her daughter's healing wasn't just about one family's miracle. It was about Jesus demonstrating that His love, His power, and His salvation weren't limited by human prejudices or cultural boundaries.

# Chapter 24

# Her Bold Plea for Her Daughter

**O**R: *HOW TO WIN A THEOLOGICAL DEBATE WITH JESUS USING NOTHING BUT MAMA BEAR LOGIC*

*"Yes it is, Lord," she said. "Even the dogs eat the crumbs that fall from their master's table."* — Matthew 15:27

### When Desperation Meets Divine Scheduling Conflicts

After years of watching her daughter suffer through demonic possession—and let's be honest, probably weeks of arguing with herself about whether chasing down a Jewish rabbi was the stupidest idea she'd ever had—our Syrophoenician mama was DONE with polite society, cultural boundaries, and anyone who thought her baby wasn't worth saving.

So she finds Him.

After everything—the sleepless nights, the long journey, the rehearsed speeches bouncing around in her head like anxious butterflies—she actually finds Jesus. And girl, you'd think this is where the story gets easy, right? Where she falls at His feet, He says some beautiful words, waves His hand, and boom—daughter healed, roll credits, everyone goes home happy.

Yeah, no.

What actually happens is so much messier and more beautiful and more *real* than any of us want to admit when we're sitting in our comfortable church pews pretending prayer is always neat and tidy.

## The Collision

Picture it: She's probably out of breath, her heart hammering in her chest, and there He is—the Rabbi everyone's been talking about. The one who supposedly heals people with just a word. The one who might be her daughter's only chance.

And she just... lets it all out.

Not the polished speech she practiced. Not the carefully worded theological argument she'd been crafting in her mind. Just raw, desperate, mother-love poured out in a public street: "Lord, Son of David, have mercy on me! My daughter is demon-possessed and suffering terribly."

Can we just stop here for a second? Because this woman—this *Gentile* woman—she's calling Him "Son of David." That's a distinctly Jewish messianic title. She's doing her homework, showing respect, acknowledging who He is. She's not coming in hot with demands. She's coming in vulnerable, using language that shows she recognizes His identity and authority.

But here's the thing about vulnerability: it doesn't always get the response we expect.

## The Silence That Screams

Jesus doesn't answer her.

Like, at all.

The text just says He "did not answer a word."

Can you imagine? You've just poured out your heart about your suffering child, and you get... nothing. Not even a "sorry, can't help you." Just silence. The kind of silence that makes you wonder if you were even heard. The kind that makes every second feel like an hour.

And while she's standing there in that awful quiet, the disciples—these guys who are supposed to be learning about mercy and grace—they start whining to Jesus: "Send her away, for she keeps crying out after us."

*Send her away.*

Not "Maybe we should help her." Not "Her pain seems genuine." Just "She's bothering us, make her stop."

(And honestly? How many times have we been those disciples? How many times have we seen someone's messy, inconvenient pain and thought, "Can someone please just... make this go away?")

## The Mission Statement

Then Jesus speaks. Finally.

But what He says is somehow worse than the silence: "I was sent only to the lost sheep of Israel."

Full stop. End of sentence. You're not on the list, lady.

Now, let's be real about what just happened. Jesus just pulled out what sounds like an official divine policy statement. The Greek word for "sent" here—*apestalin*—that's the language of official commissions. It's governmental. It's "I have orders from headquarters." It's not personal, it's protocol.

And any reasonable person would have heard that and thought, "Okay, I tried. This was a long shot anyway. Time to go home and figure out plan B."

But this woman? She doesn't even flinch.

## The Worship That Looks Like Wrestling

Instead of leaving, she comes *closer*.

The text says she "came and knelt before him." She's literally getting down on the ground in front of Him. And she says just three words: "Lord, help me!"

Strip away everything else—the theology, the policy, the Jewish-Gentile divide—and what you have left is the most honest prayer ever prayed: *Lord, help me.*

This is the prayer underneath all our prayers. The one we're really praying when we dress it up in fancier language. The cry that every parent who's ever watched their child suffer knows in their bones.

She's worshiping Him even while He seems to be saying no. She's honoring Him even as He appears to be rejecting her. That's not denial—that's faith that sees past the immediate to something bigger.

## The Dog Statement

And this is where Jesus says something that, if we're being honest, makes us really uncomfortable.

"It is not right to take the children's bread and toss it to the dogs."

Children = Jews. Dogs = Gentiles. Do the math.

Now before we get all scandalized, we need to understand something: the word Jesus used for "dogs" here—*kynaria*—isn't talking about the mangy street mutts that would attack you in an alley. It's the word for household puppies. Little pets. The dogs that hang around under the table during dinner hoping for dropped food.

But still. *Dogs.*

Most of us would have been out of there. Like, "Okay, I came here for healing and I'm leaving with trauma. Thanks for nothing, Rabbi."

But watch what she does with this.

## The Comeback That Changed Everything

"Yes it is, Lord," she said. "Even the dogs eat the crumbs that fall from their master's table."

OH. MY. WORD.

Do you see what she just did? She took His metaphor—the one that seemed designed to shut her down—and she *ran with it.* She didn't get offended. She didn't argue with His mission statement. She didn't try to prove she was better than a dog.

She just said, "Okay, I'm a dog in this analogy. Fine. But even the dogs in Your house get fed."

She agreed with the hierarchy (*Yes, the children eat first*), acknowledged His authority (*Yes, Lord*), but then pointed out the beautiful, undeniable truth: In a good master's house, even the pets are cared for. There's always enough. The crumbs alone would be more than sufficient for what she needs.

And here's the sneaky brilliant part: by accepting the dog label, she's actually claiming membership in the *household*. She's not positioning herself as a stranger begging at the door. She's saying, "I'm part of Your family, even if I'm the family pet. And family takes care of family."

The wordplay is genius. The theology is sound. The faith is staggering.

She's basically saying, "I don't need to be at the table. I don't need the full feast. Just a crumb of Your power—just the overflow of what You're doing for Israel—that's more than enough to heal my daughter."

### The Moment Everything Shifts

And Jesus—who probably had the biggest smile on His face at this point—He says something that must have made the disciples choke on their own assumptions:
"Woman, you have great faith! Your request is granted."

## Great faith.

Not "okay faith" or "pretty good faith" or even "impressive for a Gentile faith."

*GREAT* faith.

He uses the same respectful term—"Woman"—that He used when speaking to His own mother. And He declares her faith *great*. Greater than most of what He'd seen among His own people. Greater than the disciples standing around watching this whole thing go down.

And then, while she's still standing there—still dusty from the road, still trembling from the emotional gauntlet she just ran—her daughter is healed. Right that second. Not "when you get home, you'll find her better." Not "in a few days, check back."

*That very moment.*

## **What Just Happened Here**

Can we talk about what this woman actually did? Because it's kind of revolutionary.

She didn't just pray for a miracle. She *negotiated* with Jesus. She engaged in what looked like an argument but was actually the most profound act of faith in the Gospels. She took what looked like rejection and found the yes hidden inside it.

She prayed like someone who understood that God's love is so abundant, so overflowing, that even the extras—even the crumbs—are more than enough to change everything.

She prayed like someone who refused to let protocol stand between her and her child's freedom.

She prayed like someone who knew that faith sometimes looks like standing your ground when everything in you wants to run.

And Jesus? He didn't just tolerate her boldness. He *celebrated* it. He held her up as an example. He basically said, "THIS. This is what I've been looking for. This is what faith looks like when it's real and desperate and unafraid to wrestle."

## The Prayer That Breaks the Mold

Because here's what we miss when we make prayer too polite, too scripted, too safe:

This woman interrupted Jesus. She argued with Him. She refused to take no for an answer. She pushed back on what looked like a divine policy. She was loud when women were supposed to be quiet. She was persistent when she was supposed to be polite. She was shameless when she should have been ashamed.

And Jesus called it *great faith.*

Not despite her audacity. *Because* of it.

She didn't pray like someone trying to manipulate God into doing what she wanted. She prayed like someone who actually believed that God's character is good, that His resources are unlimited, and that His love extends even to the ones who don't fit the usual categories.

She prayed like a girl who refused to let anyone—not social convention, not religious boundaries, not even an apparent "no" from Jesus Himself—stand between her and the miracle her daughter needed.

And in doing so, she didn't just get her miracle.

She rewrote the rules for everyone who came after her.

She proved that God's table is bigger than we think. That His love spills over boundaries we thought were fixed. That persistence isn't presumption—it's faith in action.

She prayed like a mother who loved her daughter more than she feared rejection.

And that, it turns out, is exactly the kind of prayer that moves heaven.

*(Now I'm off to practice my theological debate skills on my houseplants)*

# Chapter 25

# Lessons from Syrophoenician Woman's Prayer

**O**R: **HOW TO TURN DESPERATION INTO DIVINE BREAKTHROUGHS LIKE A BOSS**

*"Daughter, your faith has healed you. Go in peace."*
— Luke 8:48

Okay, so we've watched this mama march up to Jesus, weather what looks like rejection, flip a metaphor on its head, and walk away with a miracle. Epic, right? But if we just say "wow, cool story" and move on, we're missing the entire point.

Because this woman—this outsider, this desperate mother, this theological ninja—she left us a masterclass in how to pray when everything's on the line. And honey, I think we need it more than we want to admit.

## *The Permission to Be Messy*

Let's start here, because this might be the most revolutionary thing she taught us: Your prayer doesn't need to be pretty to be powerful.

I don't know about you, but I grew up thinking prayer had to sound a certain way. You know the tone—that special "prayer voice" people use where they suddenly sound like they're narrating a documentary about Jesus. Formal. Measured. Theologically correct. Like if you use the wrong words or forget to say "in Jesus' name" at the end, God's going to hit delete on your request.

The Syrophoenician woman blew that whole idea out of the water.

She didn't show up with flowery language or a carefully constructed theological argument. She showed up desperate, loud, and kind of rude by first-century standards. She interrupted. She persisted even when told to go away. She argued with Jesus—*argued with Him*—using His own words against Him in the most brilliant way possible.

And Jesus loved it.

He didn't say, "Woman, you need to calm down and approach Me with more reverence." He said, "Your faith is *great*."


## *The Power of Strategic Focus*

But here's where the Syrophoenician woman teaches us something subtle and brilliant: Being authentic doesn't mean being distracted.

Because let's be honest—when Jesus essentially called her a dog, she had every reason to get offended. Can you imagine? You've walked miles to find this Rabbi. You've put your pride on the line by approaching Him in public. You've poured out your heart about your suffering daughter. And His response includes a metaphor that puts you in the category of household pets.

Most of us would've gotten derailed right there. We would've started defending our worth, arguing about fairness, or storming off to find someone who appreciated us more. And you know what? None of those responses would've healed her daughter.

She could've been right to be offended. She could've had a very justified emotional reaction. But she was too focused on her goal to let offense steal her miracle.

This is huge for us. Because how many times have we gotten so caught up in how someone made us feel that we completely lost sight of what we were actually trying to accomplish? How many prayers have we abandoned because someone questioned whether we deserved an answer? How many breakthroughs have we walked away from because the path to get there required us to swallow our pride?

Proverbs 4:23 tells us to "guard your heart, for everything you do flows from it." I used to think that meant building walls to keep out anything that might hurt. But watching this woman, I think it means something different. It means protecting your heart from *distractions*—even justified ones—that would keep you from your purpose.

She guarded her heart by refusing to let offense take up residency there. She had a mission, and nothing—not social customs, not religious boundaries, not even a seemingly harsh word from Jesus—was going to derail her from it.

## The Art of Holy Boldness

Now, let's talk about persistence, because this is where a lot of us get confused. We've been taught that faith means accepting God's will with quiet resignation. If He says no, we should just nod, say "Your will be done," and move on with our lives like good little Christians.

But that's not what Jesus taught.

Remember the parable of the persistent widow in Luke 18? There's this woman who keeps showing up at a judge's office demanding justice. The judge doesn't care about God or people, but he finally gives her what she wants because—and this is literally what the text says—"she keeps bothering me" (Luke 18:5).

And Jesus tells this story to teach us that we should "always pray and not give up" (Luke 18:1).

Wait, what? Jesus used a story about annoying someone into submission to teach us how to pray?

Yes. Yes, He did.

The Syrophoenician woman understood this. When the disciples said, "Send her away, she's bothering us," she didn't take that as her cue to leave. She doubled down. When Jesus gave her what sounded like a clear no, she heard it as an invitation to negotiate.

And here's the thing—Jesus didn't just tolerate her persistence. He celebrated it. He held her up as an example of great faith. He basically said, "THIS. This is what I've been waiting for. Someone who believes enough to fight for it."

So let's get practical about what this means for your prayer life.

When you pray for something and it feels like heaven is silent, that's not necessarily God saying no. It might be God saying, "Show Me how much you believe I'm good and My resources are unlimited." It might be God creating space for your faith to grow from "I hope this works" to "I know You're able."

Matthew 7:7 puts it this way: "Ask and it will be given to you; seek and you will find; knock and the door will be opened to you." In the original Greek, those verbs are in the present continuous tense—meaning keep asking, keep seeking, keep knocking. It's not a one-and-done kind of prayer. It's persistent, ongoing, refusing-to-give-up prayer.

## *The Strategy of Using God's Own Words*

Now we need to talk about what might be the most brilliant part of her entire approach: She used Jesus' own words to make her case.

When He said it wasn't right to take the children's bread and give it to the dogs, she didn't argue with the premise. She didn't try to convince Him that she wasn't really a dog. She accepted the entire metaphor and then found the yes hidden inside the no.

"Even the dogs eat the crumbs that fall from their master's table."

This is next-level prayer strategy, friends.

She basically said, "You're right—the children eat first. But in a house where the master is good, where the table is abundant, even the pets are fed. So I'm not asking for something outside Your character—I'm asking for something that's completely consistent with who You are."

This is how we're supposed to pray. Not by trying to convince God to act against His nature, but by aligning our requests with His character and calling Him to be who He already is.

When you're praying for healing, you're not trying to twist God's arm to do something He's reluctant to do. You're reminding yourself (and declaring to the universe) that God is a Healer. "By His wounds we are healed" (Isaiah 53:5). It's not manipulation—it's remembering who He is.

When you're praying for provision, you're not begging a stingy God to loosen His purse strings. You're operating from the truth that "my God will meet all your needs according to the riches of his glory in Christ Jesus" (Philippians 4:19). You're not asking Him to be something He's not—you're asking Him to be exactly who He's always been.

When you're praying for breakthrough, you're not hoping He'll make an exception to His usual behavior. You're standing on the promise that He "is able to do immeasurably more than all we ask or imagine, according to his power that is at work within us" (Ephesians 3:20).

Get familiar with who God says He is in Scripture. When you pray, use His own words. Remind Him (and yourself) of His promises. That's not being presumptuous—that's being smart.

## *The Reality Check: This Doesn't Mean God Always Says Yes*

Okay, we need to have a real conversation here, because I don't want you to walk away from this chapter thinking that if you just pray boldly enough, God will give you whatever you want like some cosmic vending machine.

That's not what this story teaches us.

What it teaches us is that God values authentic, persistent, bold faith. It teaches us that He's not intimidated by our intensity or offended by our honesty. It teaches us that barriers we think are fixed are actually movable when faith shows up.

But it doesn't promise that every prayer will be answered exactly the way we want, on the timeline we demand.

Here's what I believe this woman's story is really showing us: God responds to faith that trusts His character even when it doesn't understand His methods. She didn't know *why* Jesus initially said no. She didn't understand the bigger theological implications of her encounter. But she knew enough about who He was to keep pushing.

Sometimes God's first answer is no because He's got something better planned. Sometimes the waiting period is where our faith gets strengthened enough to handle the breakthrough we're asking for. Sometimes the miracle we're demanding isn't the miracle we actually need.

But here's what I know for sure: When we show up with genuine faith, when we refuse to let offense or fear or doubt derail us, when we're bold enough to use God's own promises as our prayer strategy—He responds. Maybe not always in the way we expect, but always in the way that's best.

Jeremiah 29:11 isn't just a pretty verse for graduation cards. It's a promise: "For I know the plans I have for you, declares the Lord, plans to prosper you and not to harm you, plans to give you hope and a future."

The Syrophoenician woman's faith didn't force God's hand. It revealed God's heart. And His heart has always been for the outsider, the desperate, the one who's willing to push past every obstacle to find Him.

## *So What Does This Look Like in Real Life?*

Let me get really practical with you for a minute.

Tomorrow morning, when you wake up and whatever situation you've been praying about is still unchanged—when the relationship is still broken, the finances are still tight, the diagnosis is still scary, the dream still seems impossible—you have a choice.

You can pray safe prayers. The kind that don't risk disappointment because they don't really ask for anything specific. The kind that are so vague and spiritual-sounding that there's no way to know if they were answered or not.

Or you can pray like the Syrophoenician woman.

You can show up honest. "God, I don't understand why this hasn't changed yet, but I'm here again anyway."

You can show up bold. "I know You're able. I've read the stories. I know what You've done before, and I'm asking You to do it again."

You can show up persistent. "I'm not leaving. I'm not giving up. I'm going to keep knocking on this door until You answer, because I believe You're good and Your resources are unlimited."

You can show up strategic. "Your word says [insert promise here], and I'm standing on that. I'm asking You to be exactly who You say You are."

And here's the beautiful part—even if the answer doesn't come today, even if you're still waiting, the very act of praying this way changes you. It builds something in you that safe prayers never will. It strengthens your faith muscles. It teaches you that God can handle your intensity, your questions, your boldness.

It makes you dangerous in the best possible way.

## *Your Invitation to the Table*

So here we are, at the end of this woman's story and the beginning of yours.

You're standing in front of Jesus right now, whether you realize it or not. He's looking at you, waiting to see what you'll do with the obstacles in front of you. Waiting to see if you'll believe that His table is abundant enough to include you, that His love is wide enough to reach you, that His power is available enough to change your situation.

The disciples are still trying to send desperate people away. The religious folks are still trying to enforce boundaries that God never set. The world is still trying to convince you that you're not qualified, not worthy, not enough.

But you—you've got a secret weapon now.

You know what the Syrophoenician woman knew: That God's crumbs are better than the world's banquets. That His overflow is more than sufficient. That His yes is bigger than everyone else's no.

So pull up to the table, friend.

Come with your mess and your desperation and your raw, unfiltered honesty. Come with your boldness and your persistence and your refusal to let offense steal your miracle. Come with your mama-bear faith and your holy audacity and your willingness to look foolish for the sake of breakthrough.

Come exactly as you are, and refuse to leave until He shows up.

Because if a pagan single mom could rewrite salvation history with one sassy prayer?

Honey, so can you.

Now go pray like you mean it.

*(Now excuse me while I go practice my theological debate skills and remind every closed door in my life that I come from a long line of barrier-breaking women.)*

# THE BLEEDING WOMAN

"If I can just touch his cloak, I will be healed."
- Matthew 9:21

# Chapter 26

# The Story of the Bleeding Woman

## "Or: How to Turn Twelve Years of Medical Bills into a Miracle"

*"If I can just touch his cloak, I will be healed." - Matthew 9:21*

You wake up one morning to find you've started your period. No big deal, right? Except this period doesn't stop. Not after a week. Not after a month. Not after a year. And definitely not after twelve bleeding years.

Welcome to the world of our unnamed heroine – let's call her Miriam, because every woman deserves a name, especially one who's been bleeding longer than some people have been alive. She's basically the ancient world's ultimate example of "when your body decides to throw the longest, most expensive tantrum in human history."

please remember Miriam is not her name but for the sake of telling her story we will name her that.

Back in first-century Palestine, women were expected to be pure, proper, and preferably pregnant (but only at the right times, obviously). Meanwhile, having any kind of ongoing bleeding made you about as welcome at social gatherings as a tax collector at a synagogue potluck.

"Meanwhile in Israel..." – Rome was breathing down everyone's necks, the religious leaders were having power struggles that would make modern politics look tame, and here's Miriam, just trying to exist while her own body has apparently declared war on her social life.

During this time, menstrual blood was considered ritually unclean according to Levitical law (Leviticus 15:19-30). Any woman experiencing irregular bleeding was essentially quarantined from normal life – couldn't touch anyone, couldn't go to temple, couldn't even sit on furniture without making it "unclean." Imagine being put in social isolation for over a decade because your body won't follow the rules.

Our girl was probably waking up every morning hoping THIS would be the day it stopped, only to face another round of "How many rags do I need to get through today?" Forget Instagram stories – her biggest concerns were finding enough clean cloth, avoiding public spaces, and watching her life savings disappear faster than discount bread at the market.

She likely spent her days:

- Calculating fabric costs like a ancient CFO
- Perfecting the art of social distancing (1,900 years before it was trendy)
- Becoming a walking medical encyclopedia as she tried every "cure" from here to Damascus
- Watching other women live their lives from the sidelines like she was permanently benched from the game of normal existence

For twelve years – **TWELVE YEARS** – Miriam had been bleeding continuously. That's longer than some marriages last! She'd seen more doctors than a medical student, spent more money than a shopaholic with a credit card, and had less social contact than a hermit monk.

The Gospel of Mark tells us she "had suffered a great deal under the care of many doctors and had spent all she had, yet instead of getting better she grew worse" (Mark 5:26). Which translates to: "The ancient medical system basically bankrupted her while making her condition worse." Sound familiar, anyone dealing with modern healthcare costs?

**Scholar's Note:** The Greek word used for her condition (*rhysis haimatos*) indicates a chronic hemorrhaging that would have been both physically debilitating and socially devastating. Some scholars suggest it could have been menorrhagia, uterine fibroids, or another gynecological condition that ancient medicine was spectacularly unequipped to handle.

**Hebrew Folklore:** There were whispers that such conditions were punishments for sin, curses from enemies, or signs of spiritual uncleanliness. Basically, victim-blaming was alive and well in ancient times. Charming, right?

### The Turning Point

Then Miriam did the unthinkable – she heard about this rabbi named Jesus who was apparently healing people left, right, and centre. Now, for a woman who'd been untouchable for over a decade, approaching ANY religious teacher was like showing up to a black-tie event in pyjamas. Completely scandalous.

But here's where our girl gets absolutely brilliant: instead of asking for an audience (which would never happen) or trying to explain her situation (mortifying), she hatches a plan that's equal parts desperate and genius. She's going to sneak through a crowd and just... touch his clothes.

"If I can just touch his cloak," she thinks, "I will be healed." Not his hand. Not his attention. Just the corner of his garment. It's the ancient equivalent of hoping you can fix your life by touching a lucky penny – except this penny happens to be the Son of God.

So she does it. Crawling through legs, dodging elbows, probably getting stepped on by half of Capernaum, she reaches out and touches the edge of his cloak. And **BOOM** – immediately, the bleeding stops. Just like that. Twelve years of medical bills, social isolation, and physical suffering... over in an instant.

## What Happens Next (Or: How to Turn a Secret Miracle into Public Theatre)

Picture Miriam's absolute euphoria – after twelve years, she can finally feel her body working normally again! She's probably trying to back away quietly, thinking she's pulled off the heist of the century, when Jesus stops dead in his tracks.

"Who touched me?" he asks.

Peter and the boys are basically like, "Uh, Jesus? You're in the middle of a crowd. EVERYONE is touching you. That's how crowds work." They're probably rolling their eyes thinking their teacher has lost the plot. Mark 5:31 records them saying, "You see the people crowding against you, and yet you can ask, 'Who touched me?'"

The Crowd is in Complete confusion. Murmuring. Probably some pushing as everyone tries to figure out what's happening. They're witnessing Jesus on his way to heal Jairus's daughter (quite the VIP emergency), and now he's stopped for... someone who touched his clothes? The crowd is probably thinking, "Can we get on with the important healing please?"

But Jesus isn't fooled. Luke 8:46 tells us he said, "Someone touched me; I know that power has gone out from me." He's not angry – he's **intentional**. He could have let her slip away, but instead he's creating space for her story to be told.

Our girl is probably having a panic attack. She went from secret healing to public spotlight in 0.3 seconds. She's trembling, knowing she's about to be exposed as the "unclean" woman who just contaminated a holy man. She comes forward "in fear and trembling" and tells him "the whole truth" (Mark 5:33).

But imagine the moment when Jesus calls her "Daughter" – the first recorded time he uses this term for anyone in the Gospels! After twelve years of being untouchable, she's not just healed; she's claimed as family. "Daughter, your faith has healed you. Go in peace and be freed from your suffering" (Mark 5:34).

## What She Might Have Done Directly After

After being publicly declared healed and called "Daughter" by Jesus himself, Miriam probably:

- Cried – ugly, happy, relieved sobbing that twelve years of pain was finally over
- Touched people – for the first time in over a decade, she could hug someone without making them ceremonially unclean
- Went to the temple – she could finally worship again, bring her thanksgiving offering, and rejoin the religious community
- Threw the mother of all celebrations – invited every woman who'd supported her through the isolation for the biggest "I'm healed!" party in Palestine
- Testified – became the ultimate evangelist, telling everyone who would listen about the rabbi who didn't just heal her body but restored her dignity

Little did she know that this one moment of desperate faith would turn her from a medical mystery into a miracle story that would be told for the next two thousand years. Her secret touch became the most beautifully public healing in the Gospels – proof that Jesus doesn't just fix our problems quietly; he makes sure everyone knows we're worthy of being called his daughters.

*Now excuse me while I go appreciate that my period only lasts a week and I have access to modern things – because twelve years of ancient feminine hygiene solutions sounds like something I definitely couldn't handle.*

# Chapter 27

# The Bleeding Woman's Silent Prayer of Touch

**"Or: HOW TO PRAY WITH YOUR FINGERTIPS WHEN WORDS FAIL YOU"**

*"If I only touch his cloak, I will be healed." - Matthew 9:21*

So here she is. After twelve years of bleeding, twelve years of being untouchable, twelve years of watching her life drain away one day at a time—Miriam is standing at the edge of the biggest crowd she's been near in over a decade.

And she's about to do something absolutely crazy.

Let me paint you the scene, because you need to feel the weight of what's about to happen. Jesus is moving through the streets, and there are people *everywhere*. Luke 8:42 says "the crowds almost crushed him." This isn't a casual gathering—this is a mob of desperate people all trying to get close to the miracle-worker they've been hearing about.

And somewhere in that chaos is our girl, trying to work up the courage to break every rule she's ever known.

Because here's the thing—Miriam hasn't touched another human being in twelve years. Not a hug from a friend. Not a hand squeeze from family. Not even an accidental brush in the marketplace. According to Leviticus 15:25-27, anyone who touched her would become ceremonially unclean. So she's been living in this bubble of isolation, watching life happen around her but never being part of it.

Now imagine what it took for her to decide that today was the day all of that would change.

## *The Desperate Calculation*

I wonder how long she stood there, watching Jesus move through the crowd, doing the math in her head. Because she was about to commit what was essentially a religious crime in broad daylight.

She knew the law. She'd been living under its weight for twelve years. By touching *anyone* in that crowd, she'd be making them unclean. By touching Jesus—a rabbi, a holy man, someone everyone was calling a prophet—she'd be doing something that could get her publicly shamed, maybe even stoned.

But then again, what did she have to lose?

Her money was gone—the Gospel of Mark tells us she'd "suffered a great deal under the care of many doctors and had spent all she had, yet instead of getting better she grew worse" (Mark 5:26). Her reputation was already ruined. Her community had already written her off. She was already living as good as dead.

Maybe that's what desperation does—it makes you brave enough to risk the little you have left for the chance at something better.

So she makes a plan. And girl, it's brilliant in its simplicity.

"If I just touch his clothes, I will be healed" (Mark 5:28).

Not his hand. Not his face. Just his clothes. Maybe if she could just reach out in this crowd, grab the edge of his garment as he passes by, she could slip away healed and no one would ever know she'd been there. No confrontation. No public shame. Just a quiet miracle and a quick exit.

She probably thought she'd worked out the perfect plan.

Spoiler alert: God had a bigger plan.

### The Touch That Shook Heaven

So she starts pushing through the crowd. And can we just acknowledge how hard this must have been? She's weak from blood loss. She probably hasn't been in a crowd like this in years, and suddenly she's surrounded by bodies pressing in from every side. People are shoving, pushing, everyone trying to get closer to Jesus.

Every person she brushes against, she's technically making unclean. Every step forward is another violation of the law she's been bound by. Her heart must have been pounding so hard she could hear it over the noise of the crowd.

But she keeps going.

Closer. Closer. There He is, just ahead. She can see the edge of His garment—those tassels, the *tzitzit*, that Numbers 15:38-39 commanded Jewish men to wear as a reminder of God's commandments. In Jewish tradition, these weren't just decorative—they were considered especially holy, representing the very presence of God's law.

And she's reaching for them. For the holiest part of His clothing. Because even in her desperation, even in her plan to sneak away unnoticed, she's aiming for the most sacred thing she can touch.

She stretches out her hand. Her fingers close around the edge of His cloak.

And everything changes.

Mark 5:29 says it happened "immediately"—εὐθέως in Greek, meaning right that second, no delay, instantaneous. "Her bleeding stopped and she felt in her body that she was freed from her suffering."

Can you even imagine what that felt like? Twelve years of constant hemorrhaging, and suddenly—silence in her body. The thing that had defined her entire existence for over a decade just... stopped. She felt it. She *knew* it. After twelve years of knowing exactly what "wrong" felt like in her body, she suddenly knew what "whole" felt like.

For just a split second, she probably thought, "I did it. I'm healed. I can slip away now."

And then Jesus stops walking.

### **The Question That Changed the Plan**

The whole procession comes to a halt. And Jesus says something that must have made her heart stop: "Who touched me?" (Luke 8:45).

Now, His disciples think He's lost it a little bit. Peter actually says—and I love his honesty here—"Master, the people are crowding and pressing against you" (Luke 8:45). Like, "Jesus, everyone is touching You. That's kind of how crowds work."

But Jesus isn't talking about the casual bumps of a crowd. He's talking about something else entirely. "Someone touched me; I know that power has gone out from me" (Luke 8:46).

The Greek word there for "power" is *dunamis*—where we get the word "dynamite." This wasn't just a gentle flow of energy. This was an explosion of divine healing power. Jesus felt it leave Him. Something significant had just happened, and He wasn't going to let it pass unnoticed.

And here's what breaks my heart and amazes me all at once: Jesus stops His entire mission to find one woman in a crowd.

He's on His way to heal Jairus's daughter, who is dying. There's a desperate father waiting for Him. Every second counts. But Jesus stops everything to have a conversation with a woman who tried to steal her healing in secret.

Why?

Because He knew she needed more than physical healing. She needed to be *seen*. She needed to be acknowledged. She needed to know she wasn't just a medical case that got resolved—she was a person, a daughter, someone worth stopping for.

### **The Moment of Truth**

So there's Miriam, trying to disappear into the crowd, and Jesus is standing there waiting. Mark 5:33 tells us she "came in fear and trembling, fell at his feet and told him the whole truth."

"In fear and trembling"—*phoboumenē kai tremousa*—she's literally shaking. This is terror. This is the moment she's been dreading. Because now it's all public. Everyone knows what she did. Everyone knows who she is. The unclean woman who just contaminated a holy man.

She falls at His feet—the position of utter humility, complete vulnerability. And then she does something amazing: she tells Him "the whole truth."

Not just "I touched You and I'm sorry." The *whole* truth. Twelve years of suffering. The doctors who failed her. The money she lost. The isolation. The shame. The desperation that drove her to break the law. Everything.

And you know what's beautiful? Jesus already knew all of it. He knew the moment she touched Him. He probably knew before she even entered the crowd. But He made space for her to say it out loud. He gave her the dignity of telling her own story.

Because that's what healing looks like when God does it. It's not just about fixing what's broken physically—it's about restoring what's been broken relationally, emotionally, spiritually.

### *The Words That Made Her Whole*

Then Jesus speaks. And oh honey, the words He chooses.

"Daughter, your faith has healed you. Go in peace and be freed from your suffering" (Mark 5:34).

Let's sit with this for a minute, because every single word matters.

"Daughter."

*Thugatēr* in Greek. This is the only time in all the Gospels that Jesus uses this specific term of endearment for someone. Not "woman." Not "sister." *Daughter.*

Do you understand what He just did? For twelve years, she's been nobody's anything. Cut off from community, from family relationships, from any sense of belonging. And with one word, Jesus redefines her entire identity. She's not "the bleeding woman" anymore. She's not "the unclean one." She's His daughter. She's family. She belongs.

After twelve years of being untouchable, Jesus gives her the most intimate title He could offer.

"Your faith has healed you."

He doesn't say "I healed you," though obviously He did. He points to her faith. He honors the courage it took for her to push through that crowd. He validates the risk she took. He's saying,

"What happened here wasn't just about My power—it was about your audacious belief that I could and would make you whole."

The Greek word for "healed" here is *sesōken*—which can mean both "healed" and "saved." She wasn't just physically restored; she was spiritually restored. She wasn't just cured; she was made whole.

"Go in peace."

*Poreuou eis eirēnēn.* This isn't just "have a nice day." This is *shalom*—complete wholeness, total restoration, perfect peace. It's the kind of peace that comes from being right with God, right with your community, right in your own skin.

"Be freed from your suffering."

Present tense in the Greek—*isthi hugiēs.* Not "you will be freed" but "be free." It's a command, a declaration, a sealing of what's already happened. Stay free. Live free. Walk forward as a free woman.

## The Ripple Effect

And then—and this is the part that makes me tear up every single time—everyone watching this unfold just witnessed something revolutionary.

This unclean woman just touched Jesus, and instead of Him becoming unclean, *she became clean*. The contamination went backward. The power flowed from Him to her, not the other way around.

That's not how it was supposed to work. Under the law, uncleanness was contagious—touch something unclean and you become unclean. But Jesus just flipped the entire system on its head. His holiness was more powerful than her uncleanness.

Which means that nothing—NOTHING—that we bring to Jesus is too messy, too broken, too contaminating for Him to handle. When we touch Him, we don't make Him dirty. He makes us clean.

The people in that crowd just watched their entire understanding of God's holiness get redefined. God doesn't stand far away demanding we clean ourselves up before we approach. He stands in the middle of the mess and invites us to reach out, knowing that His power to restore is greater than our power to contaminate.

## *What Happened Next*

Picture Miriam standing there, no longer shaking with fear but probably shaking with joy. Jesus keeps moving toward Jairus's house (because yes, He still healed that little girl—He's God, He can do multiple miracles in one day). But Miriam is left standing in that crowd, and now everyone is looking at her.

But they're not looking at "the unclean woman" anymore. They're looking at the woman Jesus called "daughter." They're looking at someone who just received a public commendation for her faith from Jesus Himself.

I wonder if people started moving toward her instead of away from her. I wonder if someone reached out to touch her hand—the first intentional human contact she'd had in twelve years. I wonder if someone offered her water, invited her home for dinner, asked if she had somewhere to stay.

Because that's the thing about being publicly restored by Jesus—it doesn't just change you; it changes how everyone else sees you too.

She probably went home to a space that had been silent for twelve years and started calling people. Started reconnecting with family. Started planning to go to synagogue again—something she hadn't been allowed to do in over a decade. Started thinking about having a future instead of just surviving another day.

## *The Touch That Became a Testimony*

But here's what really gets me: Her story didn't end in that moment. It kept going. It spread. Mark wrote it down. Luke included it in his Gospel. Matthew recorded it. Which means her quiet, desperate touch became one of the most famous healing stories in human history.

The woman who tried to sneak away unnoticed became an example for billions of people across thousands of years. Her faith—the kind that pushed through crowds and broke rules and reached out even when it seemed crazy—has been inspiring desperate people to reach for Jesus ever since.

She thought she was just trying to get healed. God knew she was writing a chapter in His story of redemption that would echo through eternity.

Because that's what God does with our desperate moments. He doesn't just fix what's broken—He turns our private pain into public testimony. He takes our secret touches and makes them into megaphones of His grace.

Miriam went into that crowd as nobody, invisible, forgotten, ceremonially dead. She came out as "Daughter"—seen, named, restored, alive.

And all it took was one touch.

One desperate, faith-filled, rule-breaking, crowd-pushing, absolutely audacious touch.

### *The God Who Stops for One*

So let's end here, because this is the truth that will wreck you if you let it: Jesus stopped for her.

He was on His way to heal a dying child—a synagogue leader's daughter, someone important, someone whose healing would have been public and impressive. But He stopped for a bleeding woman in the middle of the road who nobody even knew was there.

He didn't have to. He could have kept walking and let her slip away healed. Mission accomplished, right?

But He stopped. Because to Jesus, she wasn't an interruption to His ministry—she WAS His ministry. The kingdom of God isn't just about doing big, impressive miracles for important people. It's about seeing the invisible ones, the ones hiding in the crowd, the ones who've been told they don't matter.

It's about stopping for the one.

That's who God is. That's what He does. He's the God who feels your touch in the middle of a crowd. Who stops everything to make sure you know you're seen. Who calls you "daughter" when everyone else has forgotten your name.

And if He did it for her—this woman with no name, no status, no claim to His attention except her desperate faith—He'll do it for you too.

So maybe the question isn't "Will God stop for me?" but "Am I willing to reach out?"

Because sister, if you're reading this and you've been bleeding in some way—emotionally, spiritually, relationally—and you've been standing at the edge of the crowd wondering if you dare to reach out...

Reach out.

Push through whatever's standing between you and Jesus. Break whatever rules need to be broken. Risk looking foolish. Risk being seen.

Because the touch that feels like the scariest thing you've ever done might just be the thing that changes absolutely everything.

*This woman just taught a masterclass in turning your deepest need into your most powerful prayer.*

## Chapter 28

# Lessons from the Bleeding Woman's Prayer

**"OR: HOW TO TURN YOUR MESS INTO YOUR MESSAGE (WITHOUT ACTUALLY BLEEDING FOR TWELVE YEARS)"**

*"Daughter, your faith has healed you. Go in peace and be freed from your suffering." - Mark 5:34*

The Bleeding Woman teaches us that sometimes the most powerful prayers aren't spoken – they're lived. Girl literally turned a crowd surf into a PhD in faith studies.

**Lesson 1: Desperation Makes You Creative.** When you've been bleeding money and dignity for twelve years, you don't send a formal prayer request through proper channels. You crawl through a crowd and touch the hem of hope. Sometimes our most profound spiritual breakthroughs happen when we stop following the "proper" way to approach God and just... reach for him.

Like when you're so overwhelmed you can't even form words, so you just ugly-cry in your car and somehow that becomes the most honest prayer you've ever prayed. God speaks fluent desperation, honey.

**Lesson 2: Faith is a Contact Sport.** Our girl didn't just think about getting healed – she literally moved toward healing. Faith without feet is just wishful thinking. She embodied what James 2:17 says about faith without works being dead, except she made it into an extreme sport.

Think about it: she could have stood at the back of the crowd thinking positive thoughts. Instead, she turned her whole body into a prayer and crawled her way to Jesus. Sometimes you have to physically show up to your breakthrough.

**Lesson 3: God Honors Audacious Faith Over Perfect Theology.** According to religious law, she contaminated Jesus by touching him. According to Jesus, she activated healing power through faith. God cares more about your heart reaching for him than your understanding of proper protocol.

Let me tell you about when I tried to apply this lesson and nearly gave myself a panic attack. I was going through a season where I felt completely spiritually dried up – like, Sahara Desert levels of spiritual drought. I kept waiting for some grand moment to "properly" reconnect with God.

Then I remembered our bleeding sister and thought, "What if I just... showed up?" So I started literally praying with my feet – taking walks and just talking to God like we were best friends catching up. No fancy words, no proper posture, just me rambling about my day while walking around my neighborhood.

Those became the most meaningful prayer times I'd had in years. Turns out God is totally fine with you treating him like your walking buddy instead of a distant deity who requires perfect spiritual etiquette.

**Lets Pray Like our Girl**

1. **Identify Your "Bleeding"** – What's been draining you for way too long? Name it. Out loud. Even if it sounds ridiculous.
2. **Get Physical** – Don't just think about praying; move toward God. Literally. Walk while you pray, reach your hands up, touch something that reminds you of God's presence. Make your whole body part of the conversation.
3. **Touch the Hem** – Find one small way to reach for Jesus today. Maybe it's reading one verse, listening to one worship song, or texting one person to ask for prayer. Don't overthink it – just reach.
4. **Expect Power** – Seriously. Expect something to shift. Not because you're magic, but because faith creates space for God to work. And honey, desperate faith? That's like creating a spiritual vacuum that God rushes to fill.
5. **Tell Your Story** – When God moves (and he will), don't keep it secret. The bleeding woman's healing be-

came public testimony. Share what God does, even if it feels small.

**For the Overthinkers:** Stop planning the perfect prayer and just start reaching. God can handle your messy approach.

**For the Rule-Followers:** Sometimes the most spiritual thing you can do is break spiritual "rules" to get to Jesus. He's more interested in your heart than your technique.

**For the Isolated:** Your breakthrough might be hidden in a crowd you're afraid to join. Sometimes healing happens in community, even when community feels scary.

**For the Exhausted:** You don't need energy to have faith. The bleeding woman was probably physically depleted, but she still found strength to reach. Your exhaustion doesn't disqualify you from miracles.

May you have the audacity to reach for what seems impossible. May your desperation become your superpower and your mess become your message. May you remember that Jesus stops everything – even urgent missions – to call you "Daughter" and celebrate your faith.

And may you never underestimate the power of a desperate woman who decides that her breakthrough is worth crawling through a crowd for.

Go forth and touch the hem of hope, beautiful. Your healing is waiting, and Jesus is absolutely here for your audacious faith.

*Now excuse me while I go practice praying with my feet and probably trip over something – because apparently spiritual coordination isn't my spiritual gift*

# LEAH

*"When the Lord saw that Leah was unloved, He enabled her to conceive, but Rachel remained childless"*
*— Genesis 29:31*

LEAH

## Chapter 29

# The Story of Leah

### "OR: HOW TO GET STUCK IN A MESSY LOVE TRIANGLE (AND STILL FIND GOD IN IT)"

*"When the Lord saw that Leah was unloved, He enabled her to conceive, but Rachel remained childless" — Genesis 29:31*

Alright, buttercup, gather 'round, because if you thought you'd heard some drama in these biblical streets, you ain't heard nothing yet. Pull up a chair, grab some comfort food (you're gonna need it), and let me tell you about Leah.

Girl, do I have a story for you.

Picture this: You're born with eyes that people describe as "lovely" (Genesis 29:17)—which in ancient Hebrew is the word *rakkoth*, and scholars literally cannot agree if this means "tender," "weak," "delicate," or "sad-looking." Basically, the Bible's version of "she has a great personality." Meanwhile, your younger sister Rachel is described as *yephat-to'ar viphat mareh*—"beautiful in form and appearance." Translation: She's got it going on in EVERY department.

You've got the participation trophy of compliments, your younger sister is basically what would happen if ancient Instagram existed and someone got verified immediately, and your dad is the kind of guy who'd sell you for a goat and a smile. Welcome to Leah's life—where everything was already complicated *before* the love triangle from hell showed up.

Back in the ancient Near East, specifically in Paddan Aram (which, let's be real, sounds like a forgotten line of IKEA furniture but was actually in upper Mesopotamia, modern-day Syria), women were expected to: marry, make babies, and not ask too many questions. Your worth was basically tied to your fertility, your husband's affection, and how good you looked in a veil.

And honey, Leah was already losing the game before it even started.

## Life as the "Other" Sister

Our girl Leah was probably waking up every morning, looking in whatever ancient bronze mirror they had, and wishing she had just a *smidge* of her sister Rachel's effortless glow. Imagine constantly being compared to Beyoncé when you feel more like you're having a permanent bad hair day. Every. Single. Day.

She probably spent her days:
Doing all the chores because, let's face it, Rachel was busy tending sheep and looking ethereal while doing it. Nothing says

"I'm the hot sister" like making shepherding look like a photoshoot.

Practicing her "yep, she sure is pretty" smile for when people inevitably praised Rachel's beauty. You know that smile—the one where your face says "I'm so happy for you" but your soul is screaming.

Trying to navigate awkward family dinners where favoritism was served hotter than the lentil stew. Picture Thanksgiving with relatives who can't stop talking about your sister's achievements while you're just trying to pass the bread.

Wishing for a love story that didn't involve her dad negotiating human beings like they were livestock at a market. (Spoiler alert: That's not what she got.)

And here's the kicker—in that culture, the older daughter was *supposed* to marry first. It wasn't just tradition; it was law. So Leah is sitting there, getting older, watching her younger sister bloom into this legendary beauty, and probably thinking, "Great, so I'm blocking her path to marriage AND I'm still not married myself. Cool, cool, cool."

Forget Instagram filters—her biggest concerns were probably finding clothes that didn't make her look dowdy next to Rachel, avoiding direct eye contact with anyone discussing marriage prospects, and generally fading into the background of her own life.

Then, like a rom-com meet-cute gone wrong, a wild Jacob appeared!

This guy—fresh off scamming his brother Esau out of his birthright and blessing (Genesis 27), running for his life from said brother who wanted to kill him, and leaving behind his mama who literally helped him commit fraud—shows up at the well where Rachel is watering her father's sheep.

And oh honey, it's instant, blinding, movie-moment love. For Rachel. Obviously for Rachel. Because of course it is.

Genesis 29:10-11 tells us that when Jacob saw Rachel, he was so overcome that he single-handedly rolled away a massive stone from the well (the kind that usually took multiple men to move), watered all her sheep, and then kissed her and wept aloud. This man literally cried happy tears at a well because Rachel was that beautiful.

Meanwhile, Leah was probably at home, not knowing that her entire future was about to be decided by a lovesick stranger who just performed feats of strength for her sister.

Jacob goes to Uncle Laban (Leah and Rachel's dad) and essentially says, "I'll work for you if you give me Rachel." And Laban, ever the businessman, says, "Sure, kid. Seven years sound good?"

SEVEN YEARS.

Let that sink in. Jacob agrees to work seven years—no salary, just labor—for the privilege of marrying Rachel. And Genesis 29:20 says those seven years "seemed like only a few days to him because of his love for her."

Awww, how romantic, right?

Except Leah is watching this whole thing unfold. She's watching this man show up and fall desperately in love with her sister within minutes. She's watching him work day after day, year after year, completely devoted to Rachel. She probably heard him talk about Rachel, saw the way his face lit up when Rachel walked by, witnessed the kind of love story she'd probably dreamed about for herself.

And she knew—she *knew*—that no one was coming to work seven years for her. No one was rolling stones away from wells for her. No one was weeping tears of joy at the sight of her.

Can you even imagine? Seven years of watching your sister be adored while you're just... there. Like an extra in everyone else's rom-com.

So seven years pass. Jacob's put in his time, done the work, and he's ready to claim his prize. The wedding day arrives, and this is where things get *dark*.

Now, in that culture, weddings were a big deal. Feasts lasting a week, lots of wine flowing, celebrations with the whole community. And crucially, brides wore thick veils that covered their entire faces. We're not talking about those cute little blusher veils modern brides wear—we're talking full coverage. You literally couldn't see who was under there.

Laban, Leah's father and a man who definitely put the "con" in "father-in-law," sees an opportunity. He's got this older daughter who needs to be married off first according to custom, and he's got this lovesick fool who's spent seven years working for free. So he makes a calculated business decision.

He swaps the sisters.

Genesis 29:23 says it simply: "But when evening came, he took his daughter Leah and brought her to Jacob, and Jacob made love to her."

Just like that. Leah, covered head to toe in wedding garments and veils, is sent into Jacob's tent on what should have been Rachel's wedding night.

Now let's pause here and think about what this means for Leah.

Did she want this? Did she have a choice? The text doesn't tell us, but knowing how women were treated in that culture—as property to be traded, with no say in their own futures—she probably didn't. Her father said "go," and she went.

Was she nervous? Terrified? Hopeful that maybe, just maybe, once Jacob saw her in the morning he might love her too? Did she spend that whole night awake, dreading sunrise?

Or—and this is the heartbreaking possibility—did she actually want this? Did she see it as her one chance to have what her sister had? To be chosen, even if it was through deception? To finally, *finally* be someone's wife instead of someone's shadow?

Then comes Genesis 29:25, possibly one of the most devastating verses in Scripture: "When morning came, there was Leah!"

The Hebrew here is *v'hineh hi Leah*—"and behold, it was Leah!" That exclamation point isn't just grammar; it's shock. It's horror. It's "WHAT HAVE YOU DONE?"

Jacob wakes up—probably hungover from the wedding feast, definitely confused—and discovers he's married to the wrong sister. Imagine ordering a Lamborghini and getting a minivan. A perfectly functional, reliable minivan that will serve you well for years to come, but definitely, absolutely, categorically NOT what you ordered.

And his immediate response? He goes straight to Laban, furious, and essentially says, "WHAT IS THIS? I worked for Rachel! Why have you deceived me?" (Genesis 29:25).

Notice anything missing from that interaction? Any thought about Leah. Any consideration for what this must be like for her. Any acknowledgment that she's a person with feelings who just spent her wedding night with a man she knew didn't want her.

Nope. Just rage at being tricked.

And Laban? Oh, Laban has the audacity to act surprised. "It is not our custom here to give the younger daughter in marriage before the older one" (Genesis 29:26).

REALLY, LABAN? You couldn't have mentioned that seven years ago? That seems like pretty important information to share before making a seven-year labor contract!

But Laban's not done. He's a businessman to his core, and he sees another opportunity. He tells Jacob, "Finish this daughter's bridal week; then we'll give you the younger one also, in return for another seven years of work" (Genesis 29:27).

So now Leah's situation is this:

She's married to a man who never wanted her and makes no secret of it. Genesis 29:30 doesn't pull any punches: "Jacob made love to Rachel also, and his love for Rachel was greater than his love for Leah."

Greater than his love for Leah? Girl, there was no love for Leah. The text literally says in the next verse that Leah was "unloved" (Genesis 29:31)—or in some translations, "hated." The Hebrew word is *senuah*, which means "hated, treated as an enemy, rejected."

Let that sink in. Leah woke up every morning in a house with her husband and her sister-wife, knowing that the man she was legally bound to for life would rather be with literally anyone else.

But here's where the story takes a turn, because this is where God steps in.

Genesis 29:31: "When the Lord saw that Leah was not loved, he enabled her to conceive, but Rachel remained childless."
*When the Lord saw.*

In a story where Leah has been invisible to everyone else—overlooked by suitors, used by her father, unwanted by her husband—God sees her. He doesn't just see her circumstances; He sees her heart. He sees her pain. And He does something about it.

God looked at this unloved woman and said, "I'm going to give you what will make you matter in this household. I'm going to give you what even your beautiful sister can't produce."

So, Leah's initial prayer life was probably a series of desperate attempts to earn Jacob's love. She kept bearing him sons, probably thinking, "Surely *this* one will make him love me!"

- **Reuben:** "Look, a son! Surely, Jacob will *see* me now!" (Genesis 29:32)
- **Simeon:** "God heard that I was unloved, so now He's given me another!" (Genesis 29:33)
- **Levi:** "Maybe *this* time Jacob will become attached to me, because I've borne him three sons!" (Genesis 29:34)

Each name, a desperate plea for affection, a whispered hope that *this* child would be the magic bullet that finally unlocked Jacob's heart. It was a heartbreaking cycle, a relentless striving for something that wasn't hers to begin with. She was caught in a spiritual trap, trying to manipulate God's blessings to win human approval Jacob was busy being Jacob, learning about consequences and unfair trades due to his own past deceptions, but Leah's path was one of trying to fill a human-sized hole with a God-sized (and very human) blessing. She spent years trying to earn love that was never her purpose.

But then something shifts. She gets pregnant a fourth time, and when this son is born, something has changed in her. Genesis 29:35: "She conceived again, and when she gave birth to a son she said, 'This time I will praise the Lord.' So she named him Judah."

*This time I will praise the Lord.*

Not "maybe now my husband will love me." Not "surely this will make me valuable." Just... "I will praise the Lord."

This is the turning point. This is where Leah stops trying to earn human love and starts accepting divine love.

And here's the kicker—that fourth son, Judah? He's the one whose line leads directly to King David. And from David's line comes Jesus Christ, the Messiah, the Savior of the world.

God took the unloved wife, the rejected sister, the woman everyone overlooked, and made her the mother of the Messiah's lineage. (Matthew 1:2-16)

Not Rachel. Leah.

The unwanted one became the chosen one in God's story.

That's right—while Rachel was busy being the "pretty one," Leah, the *unwanted* wife, became the matriarch of the Messiah's bloodline.

*(Now i'm off to go side-eye every "consolation prize" moment in my life—because apparently, God's best blessings start in the places we feel most overlooked.)*

# Chapter 30

# Leah's Heart in the Names of Her Children

**"OR: HOW TO TURN BABY NAMES INTO PRAYER JOURNALS (WHILE YOUR HUSBAND IGNORES YOU)"**

*"This time I will praise the Lord." So she named him Judah. Then she stopped having children.* — Genesis 29:35

After three sons and approximately zero percent increase in Jacob's affection meter, Leah was absolutely DONE with the "maybe this baby will make him love me" strategy. Picture her, probably sleep-deprived, covered in ancient baby spit-up, watching Jacob make googly eyes at Rachel across the tent while she's literally raising his dynasty single-handedly.

Girl had been trapped in a marriage that started with deception, continued with rejection, and was seasoned daily with the special torture of watching your husband treat your sister like she hung the moon while treating you like expired milk. For years, she'd been living the ultimate "pick me" nightmare—except instead of embarrassing herself on social media, she was naming human beings after her desperation.

What finally broke her into legendary prayer territory? Probably the moment she realized she was pregnant again and her first thought wasn't *"Maybe Jacob will finally love me"* but *"You know what? God's been faithful this whole time, and I've been too busy chasing fool's gold to notice."*

Maybe it was watching Rachel's continued barrenness while her own womb kept blessing her with sons. Maybe it was finally understanding that Jacob's love was never the prize—God's love was. Or maybe she just got tired of naming her kids after her emotional baggage and decided to try gratitude for once.

*Fun Bible Fact:* The name "Judah" (יְהוּדָה) comes from the Hebrew root *yadah*, meaning "to praise" or "to give thanks." Leah literally turned her fourth son into a walking worship service.

This wasn't some polite *"bless this food and keep us safe"* prayer—this was a four-part theological evolution told through baby announcements. Let's break down Leah's prayer journey, one son at a time:

## Prayer #1: Reuben (רְאוּבֵן) - "See, a Son!"

*"It is because the Lord has seen my misery. Surely my husband will love me now."* — Genesis 29:32

The Heart Behind It: Pure, desperate hope that visibility equals love. The Hebrew name literally means "Look! A son!" like she's waving a biological trophy at Jacob saying, *"NOTICE ME NOW!"*

Modern Translation: *"God, you saw how miserable I am, so you gave me this baby to fix my marriage, right? RIGHT?"*

The Problem: She's treating God like a cosmic vending machine—insert suffering, receive love tokens.

### Prayer #2: Simeon (שִׁמְעוֹן) - "Heard"

*"Because the Lord heard that I am not loved, he gave me this one too."* — Genesis 29:33

The Heart Behind It: Escalation tactics. If one son didn't work, maybe TWO will get Jacob's attention. The name comes from *shama*, meaning "to hear."

Modern Translation: *"Okay God, you HEARD my problem and you're clearly trying to help me win this man over. Keep 'em coming!"*

The Problem: She's still convinced God's main job is to make Jacob love her.

### Prayer #3: Levi (לֵוִי) - "Attached"

*"Now at last my husband will become attached to me, because I have borne him three sons."* — Genesis 29:34

The Heart Behind It: Mathematical desperation. Three sons = husband attachment, obviously. The name means "joined" or "attached."

Modern Translation: *"Third time's the charm, right God? Surely Jacob can't ignore THREE sons!"*

The Problem: She's treating children like spiritual leverage instead of blessings.

## Prayer #4: Judah (יְהוּדָה) - "Praise"

*"This time I will praise the Lord."* — Genesis 29:35

The Heart Behind It: BOOM. The prayer pivot that changed everything. No mention of Jacob. No bargaining. Just pure, unadulterated praise.

Modern Translation: *"You know what? Forget Jacob. God, YOU'VE been faithful through this whole mess. This baby isn't about earning love—it's about celebrating the love I already have."*

The Breakthrough: She finally realized God's love wasn't conditional on Jacob's affection.

When Leah probably prayed through her first three sons like, *"God, surely Jacob will love me now!"*

God's response: *"Sweet daughter, I'm giving you these sons because I see your pain—not to win someone else's approval."*

When she finally shifted to praise with Judah:
God's response: *"NOW we're talking! Watch what I do with a heart that praises Me for who I am, not for what others do."*

While Leah was desperately trying to earn Jacob's love, God was positioning her as the mother of the priestly tribe (Levi) and the royal line (Judah). Her "consolation prizes" became the foundation of Israel's spiritual and political leadership.

He didn't just bless Leah's shift from desperation to praise—He rewrote salvation history through it.
*"This time I will praise the Lord"* became the moment God said, *"Hold my manna and watch this."*

## Judah's Legacy:

- King David descended from Judah (1 Chronicles 2:1-15)
- Jesus Christ came through Judah's line (Matthew 1:1-16)
- The Lion of Judah (Revelation 5:5) traces back to Leah's fourth son

## Meanwhile, Rachel's sons?

- Joseph: Important, yes, but his story ends with his descendants
- Benjamin: Significant tribe, but not the Messianic line

*Divine Irony Level: MAXIMUM.* The "unloved" wife became the matriarch of the Messiah, while the "beloved" wife's lineage faded into the background of eternity.

The word *yadah* (praise) that Leah used doesn't just mean saying nice things about God. It literally means:

- To throw or cast (like casting your cares)
- To confess or acknowledge (recognizing God's character)
- To give thanks with extended hands (physical worship)

Leah's prayer with Judah was a full-body surrender—she threw her need for Jacob's approval at God's feet and lifted her hands in acknowledgment that God's love was enough.

Here's what Leah discovered that we often miss: When you stop praying for people to change and start praising God for who He is, you become the change the world needs.

Her first three prayers: *"God, make Jacob love me."* Her fourth prayer: *"God, I love You regardless."*

The difference? The first three were manipulation disguised as faith. The fourth was worship disguised as a baby name.

Which brings us to the revolutionary truth Leah stumbled into: Your worst rejection might be God's best redirection. She thought she was failing at being loved by Jacob, but she was actually succeeding at being positioned by God.

Her story proves that sometimes God uses our Plan B to deliver His Plan A—and honey, His Plan A always includes making you the ancestor of something bigger than your current disappointment.

### The Ongoing Battle

But we need to be real here—Leah's story doesn't end with Judah's birth and suddenly everything is perfect. Life isn't a fairy tale, and Leah's wasn't either.

She continues to compete with Rachel for Jacob's affection. There's a whole weird subplot involving mandrakes (Genesis 30:14-16) where Leah literally negotiates with Rachel to sleep with Jacob for the night. Let that sink in—she has to bargain with her sister for time with her own husband.

She has more children—two more sons and a daughter. With each one, she's still hoping, still trying, still believing that maybe *this* will be the thing that makes Jacob love her.

She lives her entire life as the second choice. The backup plan. The wife he was tricked into marrying.

And it probably never really got better. There's no verse that says "and then Jacob finally loved Leah." No moment where he looks at her and realizes what he's had all along. No rom-com ending where the guy sees the beauty that was there the whole time.

But here's what did happen: God saw her. God heard her. God opened her womb when Rachel's was closed. God gave her sons who would become the foundation of entire tribes of Israel. God put her in the direct lineage of the Messiah.

And when Jacob died, guess where he asked to be buried? "Bury me with my fathers in the cave in the field of Ephron the Hittite... There Abraham and his wife Sarah were buried, there Isaac and his wife Rebekah were buried, and there I buried Leah" (Genesis 49:29-31).

There I buried Leah. Not Rachel—she was buried on the road to Bethlehem. Leah was the one laid to rest in the family tomb, next to the patriarchs and matriarchs of Israel.

The unloved wife got the place of honor in death that she never got in life.

Leah didn't get the earthly love story she wanted. But she got something better: She got to be part of God's story. And in that story, the unloved become beloved, the rejected become chosen, and the overlooked become essential.

So buckle up, buttercup. Because now that you know Leah's story, we're about to dive into her prayers—the desperate, honest, heartbreaking prayers of a woman who learned that God's love is better than being someone's first choice.

And if you've ever felt like Leah—unwanted, unseen, not enough—Remember we serve a God who sees.

*(I'm off to rename my houseplants after Bible characters—apparently baby names carry more spiritual weight than I thought, and I need all the prayer help I can get.)*

# Chapter 31

# Lessons from Leah's Prayer

**"OR: HOW TO STOP CHASING FOOL'S GOLD AND START MINING FOR HEAVEN'S TREASURE"**

*"Cast all your anxiety on him because he cares for you." — 1 Peter 5:7*

Leah teaches us that the moment you stop trying to earn love and start celebrating the love you already have, God rewrites your entire storyline—and probably throws in a Messiah for good measure.

Look, honey, this woman spent three pregnancies treating God like a cosmic matchmaker, basically praying, *"Dear God, please make Jacob notice me exists as more than just Rachel's less attractive sister."* Then with baby number four, she had her come-to-Jesus moment (literally) and said, *"You know what? Forget Jacob. God, YOU'RE faithful, and that's enough."*

**BOOM.** That baby became the ancestor of Jesus. While she was busy chasing horizontal approval, God was busy setting up vertical legacy. Talk about divine plot armor!

## Truth #1: Your Desperation Is Not Your Destination

Leah's first three sons were basically named after her emotional baggage:

Girl was out here naming humans after her therapy sessions! But here's the kicker—God used even her desperate prayers to position her for greatness. Sometimes our messiest seasons are just God's way of preparing us for our greatest assignments.

It's like spending three years stress-eating while praying for your ex to come back, only to realize God was using that time to make you emotionally available for your actual soulmate. Except Leah's "actual soulmate" was recognizing God's love, and her reward was becoming the great-great-grandmother of the Savior of the world.

## Truth #2: Praise Is the Ultimate Plot Twist

The Hebrew word *yadah* (Judah's name root) means both "to praise" AND "to cast" or "throw." Leah literally learned to throw her cares at God's feet while lifting her hands in worship. She discovered that casting and praising are the same spiritual motion—you let go of what's weighing you down so you can lift up what lifts you up.

We'll spend money on therapy, yoga retreats, and essential oils to learn how to "let go," when Leah figured out the secret 4,000 years ago—name your problems after God's faithfulness instead of your frustrations.

## Truth #3: God's Favorite Plot Twists Start in Rejection

While Rachel was getting all the Instagram-worthy love story moments, Leah was getting the eternal storyline. God took the "unwanted" wife and made her the matriarch of the Messiah. Meanwhile, Rachel's sons? Important, sure, but not Messianic line.

Jacob spent 14 years working for Rachel, but it was Leah's fourth son who ended up on Jesus' family tree. Sometimes God's "no" to what you want is really His "WAIT UNTIL YOU SEE WHAT I'VE GOT PLANNED."

Turns out you can't just skip to the praise part without dealing with the casting part. I was trying to praise God while still white-knuckling my deepest desire. It's like trying to clap while holding onto a cactus—painful and ineffective.

As I mentioned before about our desire to have children, after we miscarried our precious baby, I found myself caught in Leah's exact same trap. Every month I'd pray, *"Maybe THIS time, God will give me a child."* I was basically naming my prayers after my desperation, just like she named her first three sons.

I finally had my "Judah moment" during one particularly ugly sobbing session. Through my tears, I surrendered that dream completely and prayed the scariest prayer of my life: *"God, if I can't have another child, please fill my home with children. Give children to everyone who steps into my home."*

It wasn't praise yet—it was pure surrender. But sometimes surrender IS the praise God's been waiting for.

Within a month, my daughter was pregnant. Month and a half later? My other daughter. Few months after that? Our daughter-in-law. In one year, three new baby additions to our family that I get to love, dote on, and pour all my grandmother affection into.

God didn't give me what I thought I wanted—He gave me something infinitely better than I could have imagined. Apparently, He knew all along I was meant to be a grandmother, not just a mother again. I just had to stop white-knuckling my plan long enough to receive His plan.

**Try This: The "Leah Challenge" (30-Day Praise & Cast Protocol)**
**Week 1: Name Your "Jacobs"**

- Write down what/who you've been trying to earn love/approval from
- Next to each one, write: *"This is not my source"*
- Practice saying out loud: *"God, You are my source"*

**Week 2: The Hebrew Throw-Down**

- Every morning, physically throw your hands up and say: *"I cast this day's worries on You"* (1 Peter 5:7)
- Every evening, same motion: *"This time I will praise the Lord"*
- **Pro tip:** Do this in your car if you don't want your neighbors thinking you've joined a cult

## Week 3: Rename Your Situation

- Instead of calling your problem by its name (*"my difficult boss," "my financial stress"*), start calling it by God's character
- *"My difficult boss"* becomes *"God's opportunity to show His faithfulness"*
- *"My financial stress"* becomes *"God's chance to prove He's my provider"*

## Week 4: The Judah Finale

- Find one person to tell about God's faithfulness in your life (even if you're still waiting for breakthrough)
- Like Leah, make your praise **public**—because when you've learned to cast and praise, you can't help but tell somebody!

## Blessing:

Sweet sister, may you develop Leah's holy stubbornness—the kind that refuses to let other people's opinions define your worth. May you learn her sacred secret: that the moment you stop chasing horizontal approval and start celebrating vertical acceptance, you become the answer to prayers you didn't even know you were praying.

May you remember that your "consolation prize" seasons might actually be God's "main event" preparations. And when life hands you the spiritual equivalent of marrying the wrong person, may you find the courage to make beautiful babies named "Praise" anyway.

May you discover what Leah learned—that the love you've been trying to earn from people? You already have it from God. And honey, His love comes with eternal benefits, a crown of righteousness, and apparently, the occasional Messiah in your family tree.

Go forth and cast those cares like you're playing spiritual basketball—aim high, let go completely, and trust that God's got better hands than you do. Your "Judah moments" are waiting, and heaven's scorekeeper is definitely keeping track.

*(Now I'm off to practice my praise-and-cast technique in the mirror—because apparently learning to let go while lifting up is harder than it looks, but infinitely more effective than my previous strategy of stress-crying while eating ice cream.)*

# MARY MAGDALENE

*"But Mary stood weeping outside the tomb. As she wept, she bent over to look into the tomb; and she saw two angels in white, sitting where the body of Jesus had been lying..."*
— John 20:11-12

# MARY MAGDALENE

# Chapter 32

# The Story of Mary Magdalene

## "OR: HOW SEVEN DEMONS, ONE RABBI, AND A BORROWED TOMB CHANGED EVERYTHING"

*"But Mary stood weeping outside the tomb. As she wept, she bent over to look into the tomb; and she saw two angels in white, sitting where the body of Jesus had been lying..."* — John 20:11-12

You're standing in a borrowed tomb at dawn, ugly-crying over your dead teacher's missing body, when suddenly two angels casually strike up a conversation with you like you're at the world's most awkward coffee shop. Then you turn around, and there's a guy you think is the gardener, but it's actually Jesus, back from the dead, and He says your name with such tenderness that your entire understanding of mortality just got rearranged.

Meet Mary Magdalene—the woman who literally went from having seven demons to becoming the first person to see the resurrected Christ. Talk about a spiritual glow-up for the ages.

Back in first-century, women were expected to be quiet, obedient, and preferably pregnant. Meanwhile, having any kind of mental or physical ailment that couldn't be explained by too much wine or too little prayer was automatically blamed on demonic possession.

"Meanwhile in Israel..." Rome was breathing down everyone's necks like that manager who hovers behind your desk, the religious leaders were having theological debates that would make modern Twitter fights look civilised, and here's Mary Magdalene, just trying to exist while her own mind has apparently been hosting a supernatural timeshare convention.

Magdala was a prosperous fishing town on the western shore of the Sea of Galilee, famous for its salted fish industry (think ancient Galilee's equivalent of a fishing village that somehow became Wall Street). The name "Magdalene" literally means "of Magdala"—so our girl was essentially "Mary from Fish Town."

Recent excavations at Magdala have uncovered a first-century synagogue with beautiful frescoes, proving this wasn't some backwater village. Mary came from money, honey—this was the ancient equivalent of living in Martha's Vineyard.

What did Mary's typical Tuesday look like before Jesus crashed her personal hell party?

6 AM: Wake up to voices that aren't her own giving unsolicited commentary about her life choices

7 AM: Try to help with family fish business while fighting supernatural mood swings

8 AM: Avoid eye contact with neighbors who whisper about her "condition"

9 AM: Attempt normal conversation, fail spectacularly when demons chime in mid-sentence

Noon: Hide during the hottest part of the day because crowds trigger episodes

3 PM: More family awkwardness as relatives debate whether to call for an exorcist or just lock her away

Evening: Collapse into bed, exhausted from fighting a war inside her own head

## Her biggest worries were probably:

- Whether she'd have a "good day" or a "seven-demons-having-a-conference-call" day
- If anyone would ever see past her condition to the real Mary underneath
- Whether her family's fishing business was suffering because of her reputation
- If she'd ever be able to enter a synagogue again without causing a scene

Galilean fishing families were often wealthy—dried and salted fish from the Sea of Galilee were exported throughout the Roman Empire. Mary wasn't just struggling with demons; she was struggling with demons while being a first-century entrepreneur's daughter.

For we don't know how long—could have been months, could have been years—Mary had been living with what Luke 8:2 describes as "seven demons." Now, before we get all spooky movie about this, let's understand what this meant in her world.

The Number Seven in Hebrew culture, seven represented completeness or perfection. Having seven demons didn't just mean Mary was possessed—it meant she was *completely* possessed. Utterly overwhelmed. The supernatural equivalent of having your computer infected with every virus known to mankind.

## What This Looked Like:

- Violent mood swings that could flip from calm to chaos in seconds
- Voices speaking through her that said things she'd never think
- Superhuman strength during episodes (think *The Exorcist* meets ancient Israel)
- Complete personality changes where family didn't recognize their Mary
- Social isolation because "demon-possessed" wasn't exactly a desirable dinner guest qualification

Imagine dealing with severe mental illness in a time when therapy didn't exist, medication was "pray harder," and your condition was seen as either divine punishment or spiritual weakness. Every day was a battle just to remain yourself.

In Jewish culture, demon possession meant:

- You couldn't participate in religious life (no synagogue, no temple)
- You were considered ceremonially unclean (no touching people)
- Marriage prospects? Absolutely zero
- Family reputation? Completely destroyed

Mary wasn't just sick—she was a social pariah in a culture where community was everything.

Then word starts spreading about this radical rabbi named Jesus who was healing people. Not just headaches or broken bones—we're talking blind people seeing, dead people walking, and demons fleeing like their lease was up.

*"Could this be real?"* Mary probably wondered during one of her clearer moments. *"Could someone actually help me?"*

Here's where it gets beautiful: While other religious leaders would have crossed the street to avoid her, Jesus saw Mary and didn't see a demon-possessed woman. He saw a daughter who needed freedom.

Luke 8:2 simply states that Jesus cast "seven demons" out of Mary Magdalene. But imagine what this moment must have felt like:

- For the first time in years, her mind was completely her own
- No more voices telling her she was worthless, crazy, or cursed
- No more supernatural episodes that terrified her family
- Complete, perfect, beautiful silence in her head—followed by peace she'd forgotten existed

*Bible Nerd Alert:* The Greek word used for "cast out" (*ekballo*) means to violently expel or throw out. Jesus didn't politely ask the demons to leave—He forcibly evicted them like a spiritual bouncer.

Here's what most people miss about Mary Magdalene's story: After Jesus healed her, she didn't just say "thanks" and go back to her old life. Nope. Luke 8:1-3 tells us she became one of the women who "provided for them out of their means."

Mary went from being supported by her family's fishing fortune to using that same fortune to financially support Jesus' ministry. She literally liquidated her privileges to follow the man who gave her back her life.

### The Revolutionary Career Change:

- **Before:** Wealthy fish heiress struggling with mental illness and Demons
- **After:** Full-time ministry supporter and Jesus' most devoted follower

Women supporting religious teachers financially was not uncommon, but women *traveling* with a rabbi's entourage? That was scandalous. Mary didn't just write a check—she left her comfortable life to hit the road with Jesus and His disciples.

### Her New Daily Routine:

- Dawn: Travel preparation (packing, meal planning for 12+ people)
- Morning: Walking dusty roads between villages
- Midday: Helping set up camp/finding lodging
- Afternoon: Listening to Jesus teach (front row seat to salvation history)
- Evening: Coordinating meals and logistics
- Night: Processing the day's miracles with the other women

Mary Magdalene is mentioned by name in all four Gospels, making her one of the most frequently referenced women in the New Testament. The Gospel writers clearly considered her testimony absolutely crucial.

What many people don't realize is that Mary Magdalene wasn't just *a* follower—she was part of Jesus' inner circle. She's mentioned first in every list of women who traveled with Him, suggesting she was their leader. Think of her as Jesus' unofficial Chief Operating Officer.

### Her Role in the Ministry:

- Financial Management: Coordinating resources for feeding and housing the group
- Logistics Coordination: Planning travel routes, securing accommodations
- Witness Documentation: Being present for major miracles and teachings
- Emotional Support: Providing stability for other women followers

**The Galilee Girl Gang:** Mary traveled with other prominent women including:

- Joanna (wife of Herod's steward—basically ancient royalty)
- Susanna (another wealthy supporter)
- Many others who had been healed and chose to follow Jesus

*Cultural Revolution Alert:* This group of women essentially created the first Christian women's ministry, traveling openly with a male rabbi and supporting His work. In a culture where women barely left their houses without male escorts, this was absolutely scandalous.

Then came the crucifixion. Picture Mary, who had already watched Jesus heal the sick, raise the dead, and demonstrate power over nature, now watching Him die like a common criminal.

### Good Friday from Mary's Perspective:

- Watching Roman soldiers nail her Savior to a cross
- Hearing Jesus cry out in agony
- Seeing the man who freed her mind now trapped in a dying body
- Wondering if everything they'd believed was a lie

*Matthew 27:56* specifically mentions that Mary Magdalene was there, watching. While most of the male disciples scattered, the women stayed. They watched their hope die one breath at a time.

Mary followed Joseph of Arimathea to see where Jesus was laid (Mark 15:47). She wasn't just a casual observer—she was memorizing every detail so she could return to properly honor His body.

Saturday Silence: Imagine Mary's mental state during that Sabbath. The man who had given her back her sanity was dead. The ministry she'd poured her life into was over. Her former life was impossible to return to. She was caught between a past she couldn't reclaim and a future that no longer existed.

Jewish burial customs required bodies to be anointed with spices within three days. Mary and the other women were planning to complete Jesus' burial preparation first thing Sunday morning.

Dawn, Sunday Morning: Mary arrives at the tomb while it's still dark (John 20:1), carrying spices to anoint Jesus' body. This isn't casual devotion—this is the desperate love of someone who refuses to let death have the final word.

The stone is rolled away. The body is gone. Angels are giving confusing announcements about resurrection. And Mary? She's having the ultimate "this makes no sense" moment.

*John 20:11* says she "stood weeping outside the tomb." The Greek word for weeping (*klaio*) means loud, uncontrolled sobbing. This wasn't delicate sniffling—this was full-body grief.

When Jesus appears, Mary thinks He's the gardener and asks where they've moved the body. She's so focused on her grief that she doesn't recognize the resurrected Christ standing right in front of her.

Then Jesus says one word: **"Mary."**

*John 20:16* tells us she immediately recognized His voice and cried "Rabboni!" (which means "my teacher"). Imagine the moment when grief transformed into joy, when death revealed itself to be an illusion, when the impossible became wonderfully, beautifully real.

Here's the revolutionary part: Jesus chose Mary Magdalene—a formerly demon-possessed woman—to be the first witness of His resurrection. In a culture where women's testimony wasn't even legally valid, Jesus made a woman His first resurrection witness.

The Great Commission, Mary Edition: *"Go to my brothers and say to them, 'I am ascending to my Father and your Father, to my God and your God'"* (John 20:17).

Mary literally became the first Christian evangelist. While the male disciples were hiding behind locked doors, Mary was running through Jerusalem announcing, *"I have seen the Lord!"*

The woman who had once been completely controlled by demons became the first person to proclaim Jesus' victory over death. Talk about a full-circle redemption story.

Church tradition suggests Mary Magdalene spent her later years in Ephesus with the apostle John and Mary, Jesus' mother. Other traditions place her in southern France, where she supposedly lived as a hermit for 30 years. While we can't verify these stories, they all agree on one thing: Mary spent the rest of her life telling anyone who would listen about the man who freed her from demons and conquered death.

## What We Know for Certain:

- She was Jesus' most devoted female follower
- She financially supported His ministry
- She was present at His death when most disciples fled
- She was the first witness to His resurrection
- She became the first person to proclaim the good news of Easter

Mary Magdalene became one of the most popular saints in medieval Christianity, with more churches dedicated to her than any other female saint except the Virgin Mary. Clearly, her story resonated across centuries.

Mary Magdalene proves three revolutionary truths:

1. **Your Past Doesn't Define Your Purpose**

    - She went from demon-possessed to resurrection witness
    - Her mental illness became her testimony
    - God uses broken people to announce breakthrough

2. **Loyalty Beats Credentials**

    - While educated disciples hid, Mary stayed faithful
    - Her devotion, not her theological training, made her a witness
    - Sometimes the best evangelists are those who know what they've been saved from

3. **Women's Voices Matter in God's Kingdom**

    - Jesus chose a woman to be His first resurrection witness
    - In a culture that silenced women, God amplified Mary's voice
    - The good news of Easter was first proclaimed by female lips

Little did Mary know that her darkest moment—weeping outside an empty tomb, convinced that even death couldn't give her closure—would become the setup for the most important conversation in human history. Her broken-hearted prayer in that garden wasn't just grief; it was faith refusing to let go, even when letting go seemed like the only logical option.

Her tears were about to become the irrigation for the greatest miracle ever witnessed.

*(Now excuse me while I go ugly-cry in gratitude that my worst mental health days aren't demon possession, and my biggest worry isn't whether the Messiah I've been following is actually still alive—because Mary Magdalene just put all my problems in perspective.)*

Chapter 33

# Mary Magdalene's Brokenhearted Prayer

**"OR: HOW TO HAVE A CONVERSATION WITH ANGELS WHILE UGLY-CRYING OVER MISSING BODIES"**

*"They have taken my Lord away, and I don't know where they have put him."* — John 20:13

Imagine it: dawn in Jerusalem. The sky still bruised from the night, the air damp with garden dew. And there's Mary Magdalene, trudging toward a tomb with a jar of spices clutched like a lifeline. She's been up all night, tossing and turning on her mat, whispering to herself: *"Okay, at least I can anoint His body. At least I can do this one last thing for Him. At least I can say goodbye."*

She wasn't prepared for this. None of them were. For three years she'd been Jesus' roadie — following Him from town to town, watching Him heal lepers with a touch, raise the dead with a word, and cast demons out with nothing but holy authority. He had freed *her* from seven demons (Luke 8:2). He'd rebuilt her life from ashes. So when she saw Him nailed to that cross, it wasn't just her Rabbi dying — it was her hope. Her future. Her sanity.

Mary Magdalene was standing in front of an empty tomb at dawn on Sunday morning, having the absolute worst panic attack in biblical history.

Sleep-deprived from three days of watching her Messiah get crucified, die, and now apparently *disappear*, carrying expensive burial spices like some kind of ancient grief-shopping therapy, and discovering that even death can't give her the closure she desperately needs. Girl was about to have a theological breakdown that would make Job's complaints look like mild disappointment.

In Jewish culture, not properly burying someone was like the ultimate disrespect. Mary wasn't just sad—she was spiritually scandalized that her Teacher couldn't even get a decent funeral.

What finally broke her into this legendary prayer meltdown? Probably the moment she realized that even her grief had been stolen from her. She couldn't mourn Jesus properly because someone had *taken His body*. It's like showing up to a funeral and finding out someone stole the casket—devastating and confusing in equal measure.

Mary had probably spent the walk to the tomb rehearsing what she'd say, how she'd honor Him, maybe even practicing her goodbye speech. Instead, she's standing there like someone who showed up to the wrong wedding, except instead of embarrassment, she's drowning in existential panic.

*"They've taken Him?"* she probably whispered to herself. *"They tortured Him, killed Him, and now they won't even let Him rest in peace?"*

The woman who had been freed from seven demons was about to discover that grief can possess you just as completely as supernatural forces—and sometimes it's harder to cast out.

This wasn't some polite *"bless you"* prayer—this was raw, unfiltered, ugly-crying spiritual desperation. Mary's prayer at the tomb was basically one long, heartbroken question mark addressed to anyone in the universe who might have answers.

John 20:11 tells us she was "weeping outside the tomb." The Greek word *klaio* doesn't mean gentle tears—it means full-body sobbing, the kind where snot runs down your face and you can't catch your breath. This was grief with no dignity, no composure, no pretty Instagram filter.

The Angels' Question: *"Woman, why are you weeping?"* (John 20:13)

Now, can we appreciate how monumentally stupid this question sounds? Two heavenly beings, sitting in an empty tomb, asking a woman why she's crying over her missing Messiah. It's like asking someone why they're upset about their house burning down while standing in the ashes.

Mary's Response: *"They have taken my Lord away, and I don't know where they have put him"* (John 20:13).

Let's break down this prayer of pure desperation:

**"They have taken"** - The Greek word *airo* means to lift up, carry away, or steal. Mary's convinced this is theft, not resurrection.

**"My Lord"** - *Kyrios mou* - intensely personal. Not "the Lord" or "our Teacher," but *my* Lord. This is possessive grief.

**"I don't know where"** - Complete helplessness. The woman who'd organized Jesus' entire ministry logistics was utterly lost.

When Jesus appears (disguised as a gardener), Mary asks the same question again: *"Sir, if you have carried him away, tell me where you have put him, and I will get him"* (John 20:15).

Mary is literally asking Jesus where Jesus is. She's so blinded by grief that she can't recognize the answer to her prayer standing right in front of her. Sometimes our pain makes us miss our miracles.

Mary's prayer connects to the Hebrew concept of *hesed*—loyal, covenant love that refuses to give up. Her determination to find Jesus' body wasn't just grief; it was the same kind of stubborn devotion that made her follow Him for three years.

In ancient Jewish culture, caring for the dead was considered one of the highest acts of love (*chesed shel emet*—true kindness). Mary was essentially praying: *"God, I couldn't save Him alive, but let me at least honor Him dead."*

While she's begging to anoint a corpse, she's actually talking to the resurrected Christ. Her prayer for closure was about to become the opening of eternal hope.

## When Heaven Uses Your Name as the Answer

When Mary probably expected the "gardener" to give her directions to the nearest morgue, Jesus pulled the ultimate divine reveal:

*"Mary."*

That's it. One word. Her name, spoken with the voice she'd heard teach, heal, and forgive for three years. The Greek text suggests He said it with the same tone He'd always used—tender, knowing, full of love.

Mary's Response: *"Rabboni!"* (which means "my teacher") (John 20:16).

"Rabboni" is more intimate than "Rabbi"—it's like the difference between "Professor" and "my beloved teacher." Mary's recognition wasn't just intellectual; it was heart-deep, soul-level knowing.

When Mary probably lunged forward for the reunion hug of the century, Jesus says: *"Do not hold on to me, for I have not yet ascended to the Father"* (John 20:17).

This wasn't rejection—it was redirection. He was essentially saying: *"Mary, I'm not staying in the same way I was before. But I'm not leaving you either. I'm going to be with you in a completely new way."*

Then Jesus commissioned Mary with the most important message in human history:

*"Go instead to my brothers and tell them, 'I am ascending to my Father and your Father, to my God and your God'"* (John 20:17).

Let's unpack this divine download:

1. **"Go to my brothers"** - Jesus calls the disciples who abandoned Him "brothers." Forgiveness included.
2. **"My Father and your Father"** - Family language. The resurrection means adoption into God's family.
3. **"My God and your God"** - Shared deity. What belongs to Jesus now belongs to His followers.

Jesus made Mary the first resurrection evangelist. In a culture where women's testimony wasn't legally valid, God chose a woman to announce the most legally important event in history.

The woman who'd been asking "Where is He?" became the first person authorized to announce "He is risen!"

## When Grief Becomes Gospel

Here's what Mary discovered in that garden: Sometimes the prayer God answers isn't the one you prayed, but the one your heart needed.

She prayed: *"Where is His body?"* God answered: *"He doesn't need one anymore."*
She prayed: *"Let me anoint Him for burial."* God answered: *"Let me anoint you for ministry."*

She prayed: *"Don't let this be the end."* God answered: *"This is the beginning."*

The Sacred Exchange: Mary came to the tomb carrying spices for a corpse and left carrying news of eternal life. Her burial preparations became birth announcements for the kingdom of heaven.

Mary's tomb-side prayer teaches us that sometimes our most desperate moments are God's setup for our most powerful purposes. She thought she was having her final conversation with grief, but she was actually having her first conversation with resurrection hope.

That thing you're mourning? That dream that "died"? That relationship that ended? That opportunity that disappeared? God might not give you back what you lost, but He might give you something infinitely better—the chance to announce His goodness to a world that needs resurrection hope.

**The Mary Magdalene Prayer Model:**

1. **Bring your grief honestly** (No spiritual makeup required)
2. **Ask your desperate questions** (Even the ones that seem obvious to angels)
3. **Stay present in your pain** (Don't run from the tomb—healing happens there)
4. **Listen for your name** (God's voice cuts through all the noise)
5. **Accept the new assignment** (Your pain might be someone else's hope)

Which brings us to the revolutionary truth Mary stumbled into: Your broken heart might be exactly what God uses to mend someone else's. Her tears at the tomb became the irrigation for the greatest story ever told.

She didn't just get her grief resolved—she got promoted to Chief Resurrection Officer. Her prayer wasn't just answered; it was transformed into the answer for everyone who would ever wonder if death gets the final word.

*(Excuse me while I go practice and pray that I will hear my name)*

# Chapter 34

# Lessons from Mary Magdalene's Prayer

**"OR: HOW TO TURN YOUR HOT MESS INTO YOUR HOLY MESSAGE (WITHOUT SCARING THE ANGELS)"**

*"Weeping may stay for the night, but rejoicing comes in the morning."* — Psalm 30:5

Mary Magdalene teaches us that sometimes God's biggest miracles are standing right in front of us, but our grief goggles are so foggy we mistake Jesus for the gardener. Girl literally had a full conversation with the resurrected Christ while asking Him where Christ was—which is basically the spiritual equivalent of looking for your glasses while wearing them.

But here's the beautiful thing: Jesus didn't get offended by her blindness or impatient with her tears. He just said her name, and suddenly everything came into focus. Sometimes the breakthrough isn't about seeing better—it's about hearing clearer.

## Truth #1: Your Worst Day Might Be God's Setup for His Best Work

Mary thought Easter Sunday was going to be the worst day of her life—showing up to anoint a dead body, accepting that her hope was buried forever. Instead, it became the day she got to announce the most important news in human history.

Remember Joseph? Sold into slavery by his brothers, falsely accused, thrown in prison—and then became second-in-command of Egypt during a famine that would've killed his entire family (Genesis 50:20). God has a PhD in turning your worst chapters into your greatest testimonies.

## Truth #2: Grief Doesn't Disqualify You from Miracles

The religious crowd probably would've told Mary to go home, get herself together, maybe take a spiritual shower before approaching the tomb. But Jesus met her in her mess—snot-streaked face, tear-stained clothes, and all.

*Hilarious reality check:* We spend more time trying to look "spiritually ready" for God than Mary spent becoming the first resurrection witness. She showed up looking like she'd been hit by an emotional freight train, and Jesus was like, "Perfect. You're hired."

Even David wrote Psalms while hiding in caves, covered in dust and desperation (Psalm 142). Some of the most beautiful worship songs in history came from a man who was literally having a breakdown in a rock formation.

## Truth #3: Sometimes You Have to Stop Looking for What's Dead to See What's Alive

Mary was so focused on finding Jesus' corpse that she almost missed Jesus Himself. She had come prepared for burial rituals when she should have been ready for resurrection revelations.

### TRY THIS: THE "STOP, LOOK, AND LISTEN" PRAYER CHALLENGE

### Week 1: The Ugly Cry Permission Slip

- Set aside 10 minutes to pray—but here's the catch: you're only allowed to tell God how you *really* feel
- No spiritual vocabulary required. If you're angry, say "I'm angry." If you're confused, say "I have no idea what you're doing."
- **Mary's example:** She didn't pretty up her grief for the angels—she just said, "They took my Lord and I don't know where He is."

### Week 2: The Name Recognition Game

- Every morning, ask God to help you recognize His voice throughout the day
- Keep a running list of moments when you sense Him speaking (through people, circumstances, even random thoughts)
- **Remember:** Mary recognized Jesus when He said her name—sometimes God's voice is more familiar than we think

### Week 3: The Sacred Stop

- When you catch yourself frantically searching for God's presence, literally stop what you're doing
- Ask yourself: "What if He's already here, and I'm just looking in the wrong direction?"
- **Biblical backup:** "Be still, and know that I am God" (Psalm 46:10)—sometimes the miracle is in the stopping, not the searching

### Week 4: The Resurrection Announcement

- Find one person to tell about how God showed up in your ordinary moments this month
- **Mary's assignment:** She became the first evangelist by simply saying, "I have seen the Lord!"
- Your version might be: "I saw God in my day to day

Here's something we don't talk about enough: Mary's prayer wasn't just about finding Jesus—it was about learning to receive news that didn't make sense. The angels told her about resurrection, but she was still looking for a corpse. Sometimes God's answers are so much bigger than our questions that we can't process them at first.

### Biblical examples of people missing God's point:

- **Martha** worried about dinner prep while Jesus was trying to teach about eternal life (Luke 10:38-42)
- **The disciples** expected a political kingdom while Jesus was establishing a spiritual one (Acts 1:6)

- **Sarah** laughed at God's pregnancy announcement because it seemed impossible (Genesis 18:12)

Maybe your prayer for a better job isn't being answered because God's preparing you for a completely different career. Maybe your prayer for healing isn't happening the way you expected because God's doing something deeper than physical restoration.

Here's the plot twist Mary discovered: Her grief didn't disqualify her from being God's messenger—it made her the perfect candidate. Who better to announce resurrection hope than someone who'd been drowning in resurrection despair?

*"Blessed are those who mourn, for they will be comforted"* (Matthew 5:4). Jesus didn't say blessed are those who have it all together. He said blessed are those who are brave enough to feel their feelings in front of God.

Your pain qualifies you, not disqualifies you, for ministry. The same tears that blur your vision today might become the clarity that helps someone else see tomorrow.

## Go Forth and Garden-Gate Your Way to Glory

Sweet sister, may you develop Mary's holy persistence—the kind that shows up to the tomb even when hope feels dead, carrying spices for a funeral that turns into a resurrection party.

May you learn to recognize Jesus' voice cutting through all the noise of your anxiety, your doubt, your "what if" scenarios, and your perfectly logical reasons why God has probably given up on your situation.

The same Jesus who called Mary by name is calling yours. The same power that raised Christ from the dead is available to resurrect whatever feels dead in your life right now (Romans 8:11).

And when you find yourself ugly-crying in your own garden moments, asking angels stupid questions about where God went, may you hear your name spoken with such tenderness that grief transforms into gospel, and your breakdown becomes your breakthrough.

May you become like Mary—so convinced of what you've seen that you can't help but run and tell somebody, "I have seen the Lord!" Even if they think you're a little crazy. Especially if they think you're a little crazy.

Because honey, the world needs more women who've had personal conversations with resurrection and aren't afraid to announce it.

*(Now go forth and mistake Jesus for gardeners if you must—sometimes the most profound revelations happen when we're looking for the wrong thing in the right place.)*

# CONCLUSION

"The Lord gives the word; the women who announce the news are a great host."
—*Psalm 68:11 (ESV)*

## Chapter 35

# Why Praying Like a Girl Matters

**"OR: HOW FEMININE FAITH REWROTE SALVATION HISTORY (ONE UGLY CRY AT A TIME)"**

> *"The prayer of a righteous person is powerful and effective."* — James 5:16

**Dear Beautiful, Messy, Magnificent Prayer Warrior,**

Let's talk about something the church has whispered about for centuries but rarely shouted from the rooftops: Women's prayers have literally shaped the course of human history. Not as a side note, not as a "special interest" ministry, but as the main event—the secret sauce that kept God's plan moving forward when everything else seemed to be falling apart.

Think about it: While the men were busy with their swords, strategies, and theological debates, the women were on their knees (and sometimes their faces) having conversations with the Almighty that moved heaven and earth. They didn't just pray *about* history—they *prayed* history into existence.

Here's what we've discovered together in this journey: Women's prayers don't just get answered—they rewrite the script. From Sarah laughing her way to Isaac, to Mary saying yes to the impossible, to the Syrophoenician woman arguing theology with Jesus Himself, women have consistently approached God with a beautiful, dangerous combination of desperation and audacity that heaven simply cannot resist.

Why? Because women pray differently.

We don't just present requests—we *pour out our souls* (hello, Hannah). We don't just state facts—we *wrestle with implications* (looking at you, Leah). We don't just accept circumstances—we *negotiate with the Divine* (Syrophoenician mama, we see you). We don't just endure seasons—we *transform them through persistence* (Anna, the 60-year prayer warrior).

Let's trace the thread through Scripture and see how women's prayers became the backbone of God's redemptive plan:

## Sarah's Laughter Prayers (Genesis 18:12-15)

She laughed at God's promise, then named her miracle baby "Laughter." Her response to impossibility? Humor mixed with faith—and God was apparently here for it. The covenant nation begins with a woman's laugh.

## Rebekah's Belly Wrestling Match (Genesis 25:22-23)

When her twins were having UFC matches in utero, she went straight to God asking, "What is this about?" God revealed the future of two nations through a pregnant woman's prayer.

## Rachel's Desperate Bargaining (Genesis 30:1)

"Give me children, or I'll die!" she demanded. Not exactly Sunday school appropriate, but brutally honest. Joseph and Benjamin, who would save Israel during famine.

## Hannah's Temple Breakdown (1 Samuel 1:10-11)

Drunk-crying in church, making vows that sounded like spiritual blackmail. Samuel, the prophet who would anoint kings and change Israel's trajectory.

## Mary's Teenage "Yes" (Luke 1:38)

A 14-year-old girl agreeing to social scandal and potential death. The Messiah enters the world.

Every major move of God in Scripture was preceded, accompanied, or followed by a woman's prayer that sounded more like desperation than devotion.

Women approach prayer with what I call "biological boldness"—we're literally designed to nurture, protect, and fight for what we love. When a woman prays, she's not just presenting a petition; she's defending her cubs, nurturing her calling, and refusing to let impossible circumstances have the final word.

**Exhibit A: The Syrophoenician Woman** (Matthew 15:21-28) When Jesus basically called her a dog to test her faith, she didn't storm off offended. She grabbed that metaphor and weaponized it: "Even dogs eat crumbs from the master's table."

That, friends, is feminine genius. We take what looks like rejection and turn it into negotiation. We take what sounds like "no" and hear "convince me." We take what feels like dismissal and make it into dialogue. I'm sure my husband loves it as much as God does.

**The Hormonal Advantage** (Yes, I'm Going There)

Can we talk about something that makes religious people uncomfortable? Our emotions are not a bug in the system—they're a feature. While men were taught to suppress feelings for spiritual maturity, women have been feeling our way to breakthrough for millennia.

Hannah's emotional meltdown produced the prophet Samuel. Mary's trembling "yes" brought forth the Savior. Mary Magdalene's ugly crying made her the first resurrection witness.

The Hebrew word for "compassion" (*racham*) comes from the word for "womb" (*rechem*). God's mercy is described in feminine, maternal terms. When we pray with our whole emotional spectrum, we're praying in the language heaven understands best.

**How Women's Prayers Shaped Nations**

Let's get historically nerdy for a hot minute, because this is where it gets really good:

**Miriam's Worship Leadership** (Exodus 15:20-21)

After crossing the Red Sea, Moses got the theological credit, but Miriam led the praise party. Her tambourine-wielding celebration became Israel's first worship service. Established women as worship leaders in God's people.

### Deborah's Prophetic Authority (Judges 4-5)

While the men were hiding from Canaanite chariots, this woman was dispensing justice under a palm tree and leading armies into battle. Proved women could hear from God and lead nations.

### Esther's Strategic Fasting (Esther 4:16)

Three days of prayer and fasting before walking uninvited into the king's presence. Saved the entire Jewish race from genocide.

### Anna's Temple Vigil (Luke 2:36-38)

Sixty years of prayer and fasting, waiting for the Messiah. Became the first person to publicly proclaim Jesus as the redeemer of Jerusalem.

Every crucial moment in Israel's history had a woman praying behind the scenes, often for decades before the breakthrough came.

### The Science of Spiritual Warfare

Here's something that will blow your mind: Women's prayers almost feel like they operate differently in the God's realm. We don't just pray *about* battles—we *birth* victories. We don't just request intervention—we *create atmospheric shifts* that make miracles inevitable.

### Case Study: The Persistent Widow (Luke 18:1-8)

Jesus told this parable specifically to teach about persistent prayer. Notice He didn't use a persistent man as the example—He used a woman who wore down an unjust judge through sheer determination. **Jesus' point:** If a corrupt human judge will respond to persistent feminine advocacy, how much more will your heavenly Father respond to His daughters' prayers?

### The Physics of Feminine Intercession

When women pray:

- **We multiply** (Hannah's one prayer produced Samuel, who anointed kings)
- **We magnify** (Mary's Magnificat amplified God's character)
- **We modify** (The Syrophoenician woman's prayer modified Jesus' mission scope)
- **We mystify** (Mary Magdalene's garden encounter mystified death itself)

Women's prayers don't just change circumstances—they change the *spiritual atmosphere* around circumstances.

Sweet sister, the same power that moved through Hannah, Mary, Deborah, and Esther is available to you right now. Your prayers aren't just personal—they're prophetic. They're not just individual—they're intergenerational.

When you pray for your children, you're shaping the next generation's destiny. When you pray for your marriage, you're rewriting family legacies. When you pray for your community, you're shifting spiritual climates. When you pray for your nation, you're participating in kingdom advancement.

### The Ripple Effect of Feminine Faith

Monica's prayers for her rebellious son gave the church Saint Augustine. Susanna Wesley's prayers for her boys gave the world Methodism. Your grandmother's prayers for you might be why you're reading this book right now.

Women's prayers have a generational half-life—they keep working long after we've stopped breathing.

Let's address the elephant in the sanctuary: For centuries, religious systems have tried to convince women that our voices are "too much," our emotions are "unspiritual," and our prayers should be quiet, private, and preferably supervised by male authority.

But Scripture tells a different story.

Miriam led worship before there were official priests. Deborah judged Israel when there was no king. Huldah authenticated Scripture when male prophets were available. Priscilla taught theology to Apollos when rabbis were plentiful.

The pattern is clear: God has always used women's voices to advance His kingdom, especially when traditional systems were failing.

Here's the beautiful, dangerous truth: Your prayers are part of an unbroken chain of feminine faith that stretches back to Eden and forward to eternity. When you pray, you join a sisterhood that includes:

- **Eve,** who first called on the name of the Lord (Genesis 4:26)
- **Sarah,** who laughed impossibility into possibility
- **The Hebrew midwives,** who prayed while saving babies (Exodus 1:15-21)

- **Mary and Martha,** who prayed Jesus back from the dead (John 11:21-27)
- **The women at Pentecost,** who prayed the Holy Spirit down (Acts 1:14)

And countless unnamed mothers, daughters, wives, and sisters who prayed in secret and shaped history in silence.

Your name belongs on that list.

## The Sacred Assignment

So here's your mission, should you choose to accept it (and please, for the love of all that's holy, accept it):

Pray like a girl who knows her voice matters. Pray like a woman who understands her access. Pray like a daughter who remembers her inheritance.

Don't let anyone tell you to tone it down, clean it up, or make it more palatable. Hannah didn't get her miracle by praying quietly. Mary didn't birth the Messiah by staying in her lane. The Syrophoenician woman didn't get her daughter healed by being polite.

They got breakthrough by being boldly, unapologetically themselves in the presence of God.

Here's what every woman who's ever changed history through prayer understood: God doesn't just tolerate our feminine hearts—He designed His kingdom to advance through all hearts.

Our intuition? That's prophetic sensitivity. Our emotions? That's spiritual radar. Our persistence? That's heaven's invitation to keep asking. Our nurturing instincts? That's intercession in action.

We don't pray like girls despite our femininity—we pray powerfully because of it.

Which brings us to the question that's been building throughout this entire journey: What happens when a generation of women finally understands that their prayers aren't just personal therapy sessions, but kingdom-advancing, history-shaping, destiny-altering conversations with the Creator of the universe?

I guess we're about to find out. And honey, heaven is ready for what we're about to unleash.

*(Now excuse me while I go call every woman I know and tell them their prayers just got promoted from "sweet and supportive" to "strategically essential"—because apparently, we've been sitting on spiritual dynamite and using it as decoration. Time to light some holy fuses!)*

## Chapter 36

# Your Prayers Count Even the Messy Ones

**"OR: HOW TO LAUNCH YOUR OWN PRAYER REVOLUTION (TISSUES OPTIONAL BUT RECOMMENDED)"**

> *"And all things you ask in prayer, believing, you will receive."* —Matthew 21:22

**Dear Future History-Maker,**

Well, here we are. You've made it through an entire book about women who changed the world by having absolutely zero chill in their prayer lives. You've met Hannah (the original drunk-crier), Mary (the teenage world-changer), Deborah (the palm tree prophetess), Esther (the strategic faster), Hagar (the desert name-dropper), Anna (the 60-year prayer marathon champion), the Syrophoenician woman (the theological arguer), the Bleeding Woman (the silent touch-er), Leah (the praise-namer), and Mary Magdalene (the resurrection announcer).

## And what do they all have in common?

Not one of them prayed "properly." Not one of them followed the religious protocol. Not one of them waited until they felt "spiritual enough" to approach God.

They just showed up—mascara running, voices cracking, hearts breaking, hopes soaring—and had real conversations with the God of the universe. And He answered. Every. Single. Time.

## So what's your excuse?

Sweet sister, if this book has done its job, you should be walking away with one crystal-clear understanding: God is not waiting for you to get your spiritual act together before He takes your prayers seriously.

He's not checking your quiet time scorecard. He's not grading your theological vocabulary. He's not timing your prayer length or judging your prayer posture. He's just waiting for you to show up and be real.

## You have permission to:

- Cry like Hannah (even if people think you're drunk)
- Say yes like Mary (even if it doesn't make sense)
- Lead like Deborah (even if no one asked you to)
- Fast like Esther (even if it's just from social media)
- Name God like Hagar (even if you make up your own titles)
- Persist like Anna (even if it takes decades)

- Argue like the Syrophoenician woman (even if it sounds irreverent)
- Reach like the Bleeding Woman (even if it breaks the rules)
- Praise like Leah (even in your pain)
- Weep like Mary Magdalene (even when angels ask obvious questions)

**Most importantly:** You have permission to pray like yourself. Beautifully, messily, authentically yourself.

## What This Really Means for Your Tuesday Morning

Let's get practical for a hot minute. Because it's all well and good to be inspired by biblical heroines, but what does this look like when you're running late for work, your kid forgot their lunch money, and you just realized you're out of coffee?

### It looks like this:

*"God, I'm losing my mind today. Help me not to lose my kids too. Also, if You could make the traffic lights cooperate, that would be great. And maybe help me remember where I put my sanity. Amen."*

### That's it. That's the prayer.

No need to dress it up with fancy language. No requirement for perfect theology. Just honest conversation with a God who already knows you're having a Tuesday and loves you anyway.

## The Challenge: Your 30-Day Prayer Revolution

Alright, beautiful. Time to put your money where your mouth is. I'm challenging you to 30 days of praying like the women in this book—which means 30 days of:

### Week 1: Hannah's Honesty Challenge

The Assignment: Pray your actual feelings, not the feelings you think you should have.

- Angry? Tell God.
- Confused? Admit it.
- Grateful? Share it.
- Overwhelmed? Confess it.

No spiritual filter required. Hannah got her miracle by being emotionally honest, not emotionally correct.

### Week 2: Mary's "Yes" Challenge

The Assignment: Say yes to one thing God's been asking you to do that scares you.

- Maybe it's having that difficult conversation
- Maybe it's starting that project you've been avoiding
- Maybe it's forgiving someone who doesn't deserve it
- Maybe it's believing He loves you despite your mess

Remember: Mary didn't understand the plan—she just trusted the Planner.

### Week 3: Deborah's Bold Leadership Challenge

The Assignment: Step into one area of leadership God's been preparing you for.

- Speak up in that meeting

- Volunteer for that ministry
- Offer to help that struggling friend
- Start that Bible study you've been thinking about

If God can use a woman to lead armies, He can use you to lead whatever He's put in front of you.

### Week 4: Anna's Persistence Challenge

The Assignment: Pick one prayer request you've been tempted to give up on, and commit to praying it every day this week.

- That prodigal child
- That broken relationship
- That impossible situation
- That dream that seems dead

Anna-level faith: Some prayers are marathon prayers, not sprint prayers. Keep running.

### When People Think You're "Too Much"

Here's the thing, honey: If you start praying like the women in this book, some people are going to think you're extra. Too emotional. Too bold. Too honest. Too persistent. Too much.

### Good.

Hannah was "too much" for Eli (until God proved her right). Mary was "too much" for her culture (until she became the most honored woman in history). Deborah was "too much" for traditional gender roles (until she led Israel to victory). The Syrophoenician woman was "too much" for the disciples (until Jesus called her faith "great").

## When they say you're too much, you're probably right on track.

*Fun Bible Fact:* Jesus Himself was considered "too much" by the religious leaders. If you're following Him closely, you'll probably ruffle some feathers too. Feather-ruffling is often a sign you're doing something right.

While you're worried about whether your prayers are good enough, here's what's actually happening in heaven:

Your whispered "help me" at 2 AM? Angels are dispatching.
Your ugly cry in the car after a hard day? God's leaning in closer.
Your frustrated "I don't understand You" prayer? He's nodding and saying, "I know, daughter. Trust Me anyway."
Your grateful "thank You for this ordinary moment" prayer? Heaven's throwing a party.

Psalm 56:8 says God keeps your tears in a bottle. Not just the pretty, acceptable tears—ALL of them. The angry tears, the confused tears, the grateful tears, the desperate tears. He's keeping them like they're precious perfume, because to Him, they are.

Sweet friend, you have no idea what you're about to unleash. When you start praying like you mean it, when you stop performing and start being real, when you approach God with Hannah's honesty and Mary's audacity and Deborah's confidence, you're not just changing your life.

You're changing your family's spiritual DNA. You're shifting the atmosphere around your circumstances. You're modeling authentic faith for everyone watching. You're joining the ranks of history-making prayer warriors.

Your daughter will remember watching you pray through crisis. Your son will be shaped by hearing you worship through pain. Your friends will be inspired by your refusal to give up. Strangers will be touched by your testimony of God's faithfulness.

The prayers you pray today might be the foundation for miracles you won't see until eternity.

### *A Final Blessing (Grab All the Tissues)*

Before we part ways, let me speak this blessing over your beautiful, chaotic, magnificent prayer life:

May you pray with Hannah's emotional honesty, never apologizing for feelings that God already knows about.

May you respond with Mary's immediate "yes," even when the assignment seems impossible and the timing seems terrible.

May you lead with Deborah's holy confidence, knowing that God doesn't call the equipped—He equips the called.

May you strategize with Esther's divine wisdom, understanding that sometimes fasting and prayer are your most powerful weapons.

May you cry out with Hagar's desert desperation, confident that the God Who Sees will never overlook your pain.

May you persist with Anna's patient endurance, trusting that no prayer is ever wasted and no waiting is ever meaningless.

May you negotiate with the Syrophoenician woman's maternal tenacity, refusing to take "no" for an answer when lives are at stake.

May you reach with the Bleeding Woman's desperate faith, knowing that even the smallest touch of Jesus can change everything.

May you praise with Leah's transformational worship, learning to name your blessings even when they don't look like what you ordered.

May you weep with Mary Magdalene's resurrection hope, trusting that your worst days might be setups for God's best work.

### And above all:

May your ugly cries become holy prayers. May your desperate whispers move mountains. May your honest questions receive heaven's answers. May your broken places become beautiful testimonies. May your messy faith make a magnificent impact.

### Go forth, beautiful daughter of the King.

Pray like you believe you're loved (because you are). Pray like you know you're heard (because you are). Pray like you trust you matter (because you do).

And when the enemy whispers that your prayers don't count, that your voice doesn't matter, that God is too busy for your small concerns—remember:

You serve the same God who stopped everything to listen to Hannah's desperate sobs, Mary's trembling yes, Deborah's battle plans, Esther's royal pleas, Hagar's desert cries, Anna's decades-long vigil, the Syrophoenician woman's theological arguments, the Bleeding Woman's silent reaching, Leah's pain-filled praise, and Mary Magdalene's grief-stricken questions.

He has time for you too.

Your prayers count. Your voice matters. Your faith moves Him.

Now go pray like the world depends on it—because it does.

**P.S.** Don't forget to keep tissues handy. Apparently, crying like a girl is one of the most powerful prayer postures ever documented, and you're about to join a long line of women who changed history through their tears, their trust, and their absolutely unshakeable belief that God is good even when life is hard.

The world is waiting for your prayers, beautiful.

Don't keep us waiting too long.

**THE END**
*(But really, it's just the beginning.)*